The History of
Lesbian Hair

The History of Lesbian Hair

And Other Tales of Bent Life in a Straight World

Mary Dugger

MAIN STREET BOOKS

Doubleday

New York   London   Toronto   Sydney   Auckland

A MAIN STREET BOOK
PUBLISHED BY DOUBLEDAY
a division of
Bantam Doubleday Dell Publishing Group, Inc.
1540 Broadway, New York, New York 10036

MAIN STREET BOOKS, DOUBLEDAY, and the portrayal of a building
with a tree are trademarks of Doubleday,
a division of Bantam Doubleday Dell Publishing Group, Inc.

The author wishes to gratefully acknowledge New Vision Technologies, Corel
Corporation, and Lasersoft, Inc., for the use of the clip-art images in this book.

Book Design by: Holly A. Block/Fleuron

Library of Congress Cataloging-in-Publication Data

Dugger, Mary.
    The history of lesbian hair : and other tales of bent life in a straight world /
Mary Dugger. — 1st ed.
        p. cm.
    "A Main Street book."
    1. Lesbians—Humor.   2. Lesbians.   I. Title.
    PN6231.L43D84   1996
    818'.5409—dc20   96-16293
                                                                            CIP

ISBN 0-385-48037-7
Copyright © 1996 by Mary Dugger
All Rights Reserved
Printed in the United States of America
October 1996
First Edition
10 9 8 7 6 5 4 3 2 1

Contents

Acknowledgments

My profound gratitude goes to Christi Booher, Brian Dynes, Keith Hampton, and Mr. Roberts for being the funniest people in the goddamn universe. Thank you to Bruce and Kandi Dugger for your love and support. Much appreciation to the *gab* boys for being so fierce, especially the very fly Malone. For providing a wealth of inspiration, my grateful acknowledgment to the Paris Tuesday Night Dart Club & Subs: Lisa & Cathy, Deb, Cathy S., the very buff Sue S., Eddie, Sue Who, Nancy, Susan, Mary & Doris, Kathryn & Lisa, Lisa G., Tom A., Tommy 3 Kings, and Jamie. My thanks to Dona and Mary Dee for laughing in all the right places while repeatedly proving there is such a thing as a free lunch. My appreciation to the ever-helpful and entertaining Meryl. And my undying gratitude to Linda Lazier for saving me from the nuns.

Finally, to my editor, Mr. Bruce Tracy, without whom this would not have been remotely possible, thank you.

For Sabrina Haake

Preamble

Charts and pictures are important. Words are important. Combine them and you produce highly important information.

I know because I used to design presentations for a business reengineering firm that regularly billed hundreds of thousands of dollars for producing charts, pictures, and words that could be understood by a five-year-old—or the average CEO.

From this enlightening brush with big business I took away one important lesson: Whatever information is being conveyed—whether it is to fire the people in your company who don't produce, or why queers are so much more fun than everybody else—it's always better with pictures.

You are holding the fruition of years of research into the queer lifestyle. Brought to you in charts, pictures, and words. Something like this would have cost you a bundle anywhere else. You got off cheap.

Have fun.

The History of
Lesbian Hair

Life

"I Know You're Just Doing This to Hurt Me..."

Mom's right, you probably did become a homosexual just to hurt her. And while we've got her all riled up, let's just see what else we can say to really get her going . . .

"I'm gay and it's all your fault"

"And I'm dating a stripper"

"And I got my nipples pierced"

"Can I move back in?"

Perhaps you're not a lesbian but you think it might be fun. Maybe you feel your life would be enhanced by always having someone with a truck, a master's degree in social work, or a softball mitt within your circle of friends. Or, possibly, you'd just really like to honk off your mom.

Do you have what it takes?
Complete the simple aptitude test below:

Yes, it does seem to be all the rage—but are you sure that lesbianism is for you?

What do you see?
A. A delivery truck
B. Your Spiegel order
C. A career opportunity

SCORING

There are no wrong answers. However, an **A** selection indicates a certain creative deficit welcome in feminist circles; **B** denotes a propensity toward Lipstick Lesbianism; and **C** suggests that you already are a lesbian.

Build Your Own Lesbian

And who doesn't want one? Imagine having your very own social worker, Canadian folksinger, sitcom star (with optional chemical dependency problem), prison matron, pro tennis player, irrational separatist who'll provide endless hours of conversational amusement, or spinster aunt to watch the kids. You decide exactly what you want your lesbian to be and we'll send complete plans!

It's So Easy!

1. Carefully measure the area where you will be keeping your lesbian (closet, rec room, forest) and include dimensions with your order.

Note: Softball players come only in six-packs, and PC woman require acreage for periodic music festivals and moon worshipping.

2. Using our patented Nature-not-Nurture chromosomal building set and common household ingredients such as patchouli, lite beer, and comfortable shoes, you'll have your lesbian molded in no time.

3. Tighten all screws and components. Hand-tighten for social workers and eccentric aunts; use a hydraulic driver to achieve maximum overtightness required for raving separatists and PC dykes.

Slap a pair of Birkenstocks on her and you're done!

We'll even include a paint-and-mix palette to reproduce over 40,000 possible skin shades, including that weird pasty white for vegans.

Depending on your lesbian requirements, we can also supply optional touches such as acoustic guitar, eighteen wheeler, or movie star "husband" for added realism!

Absolutely free! Special female-to-female plug/outlet recharger included.

Many, Many Styles Available

Decorative Lipstick Lesbian

Best Darn Mechanic You've Ever Had

Military Clearance Sale—Build Your Own Army!

Professional Sports Figure

Coming Soon...
Build Your Own Gay Man!

Our designers are currently working on developing the most popular styles, including do-it-yourself art directors, hairstylists, and professional whiners.

The Downside to Lesbian Chic

With the escalation of Lesbian Chic, there's been a proportionate rise in straight couples trolling the lesbian bars for a three-way. A hetro manifestation in a queer bar is easily identified by three criteria: 1) the male, in an attempt to maintain the appearance of a swingin'—*straight*—guy, will rigorously avoid eye contact with anything that might even possibly have a penis, including drag queens and butch dykes, 2) the female will sport a high hairstyle that is not currently sanctioned by the Lesbian Board of Haircuts, and 3) the lesbian they are hitting on will have upped her drink preference substantially, as she is not the one paying. She will be the one drinking the pitcher of Grand Marnier.

Indeed, every decade has a status symbol to determine the alpha couple, and as we look across time we can see that the '90s are shaping up to be no different:

The '60s:
"This is our maid, Manuella"
The '70s:
"This is Binky, our Lhasa apso"
The '80s:
"This is the Beemer mechanic, Hans"
The '90s:
"This is Nancy, our lesbian"

Unfortunately for status-seeking straights, lesbians don't appear to be any more interested in hetro three-ways than we've ever been—that is to say, not at all. Not that gays have ever found straights to be overly smart, but why do they go to lesbian bars searching for the missing link to a threesome? If common sense is at all a priority for them, perhaps they would do well to look among our gay brethren to Aristotle and his contribution to the modern age: two thousand years of logical reasoning.

Using what appears to be the breeder premises of deductive reasoning, let's work out a syllogism, shall we?

Women in a same-sex environment are sexually ravenous;

the most sexually ravenous women are those who don't have heterosexual sex;

therefore, the ideal place to round out a threesome is a convent.

There: proof positive that annoying the local fauna at a dyke bar is going to garner the straight couple nothing but a deepening reputation for stupidity. It is this kind of action that only confirms the troubling image I have of breeders stumbling through life forever asking the video store clerk for ten dollars on pump no. 3, and expecting to buy groceries at the library.

If you are the male component of a trendy straight couple, you've no doubt recently said to a known lesbian, "So, are you interested in going home with me and my wife?" And if you're a known lesbian you've no doubt increasingly been jarred by a question that translates into, "Hey, the wife and I are wondering if you'd come back to our place. We're probably two of the most self-absorbed people you'll ever meet and we can't think of anything more narcissistically fulfilling than having a confirmed lesbian vying for our amorous attentions—unless of course you're not opposed to inviting the dog into it. Whaddaya say?"

I feel there are only three answers to this stupidest of stupid questions ever uttered in a lesbian bar:

"Gee, okay. I'll share you with your wife, since, you know, I'm only a lesbian because it's so damn hard to find a man that wants to have sex."

or

Look him over completely and say, with absolute conviction, "Listen buddy, you don't ever, *ever* want a woman to sleep with your wife."

or

Depending on your priorities, "Buy me another drink and maybe I'll think about it."

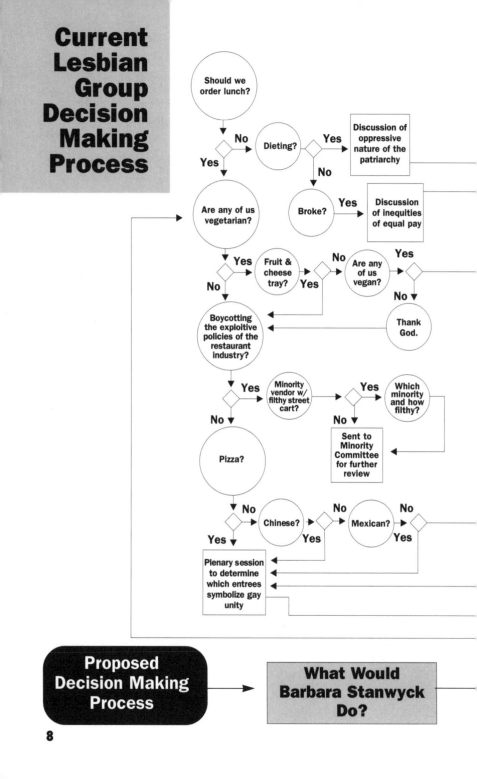

Current
Lesbian
Group
Decision
Making
Process

Should we order lunch?

No → Dieting? → Yes → Discussion of oppressive nature of the patriarchy

Yes

No

Broke? → Yes → Discussion of inequities of equal pay

Are any of us vegetarian?

Yes → Fruit & cheese tray? → No → Are any of us vegan? → Yes

No → Yes

No ↓

Boycotting the exploitive policies of the restaurant industry? ← Thank God.

Yes → Minority vendor w/ filthy street cart? → Yes → Which minority and how filthy?

No ↓

No ↓

Pizza?

Sent to Minority Committee for further review

No → Chinese? → No → Mexican? → No

Yes ↓

Yes

Yes

Plenary session to determine which entrees symbolize gay unity

Proposed Decision Making Process → What Would Barbara Stanwyck Do?

8

Rome wasn't built in a day, and a unanimous lesbian decision won't be made in our lifetime. In a group setting we form a diversity-biosphere where every teeny-tiny minority point is incubated and allowed to mature into full-grown considerations. Then we spend an eternity discussing their impact. Finally, we spend another aeon arguing inane hypotheticals.

Making a decision, any decision, deducts hours of social growth and real-life skills from the average lesbian life. Damaging? My God, yes! Curable? Perhaps . . .

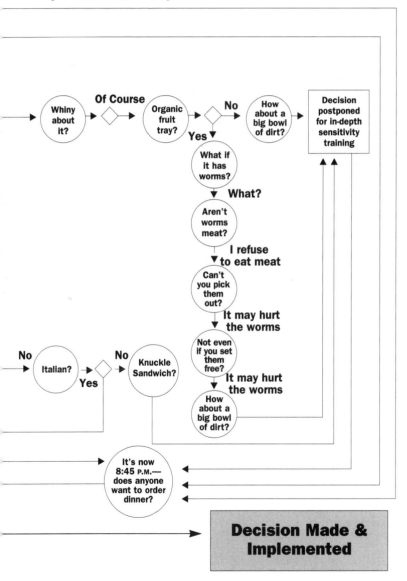

Propagation

There are only two categories of children: the ones you are related to, and the product of other people's stunning arrogance in insisting their genetic line is worth perpetuating.

Children are essentially pets with thumbs. As the consummate pet owners, gays especially should remember this. We have reached a point in our culture where many of us are deciding to obtain children. Part of that decision making process should be a determination of parental aptitude. You can discover volumes of information about the kind of parent you'll be by analyzing how well-behaved your pets are. For example, my dog feels that she should be the only dog allowed within the city limits. She expresses this by running down and attempting to kill anything that looks even vaguely doglike, including carriage horses and park statuary. I know that if she had thumbs, she would own a gun. I also know that if I were a parent, my children would be an integral part of the FBI wall at the post office.

I'll not have children.

Based on experiences with other people's children, however, I do have a few things to impart:

You will never win an argument with a willful child. Why? *Because they have no agenda.* Should you plan to get the little nipper up early Saturday morning, dress, have breakfast, visit the aquarium, then enjoy a pleasant picnic in the park, you must realize that you are doing this in association with a being that has no concept of time, let alone planning. Thus, if they refuse to comb their hair, the ensuing argument *becomes* their agenda. Their schedule leaves them quite free to throw a tantrum well into the afternoon. They don't care that the aquarium becomes hopelessly crowded after 11:00 A.M. They don't even know what the aquarium is.

As you are driving little disheveled Jane or Johnny to the aquarium, you will be glowering. They will be happily singing songs about color. As the tiny Napoleons of your universe, they have not only escaped the house without brushing a single part of their person, but are now on their way to something called an aquarium, followed by a trip to FAO Schwarz where they may choose their reward for simply agreeing not to cry anymore.

This is not to say that one can't have creative fun with children. If you start early enough, there is a good chance that by age six they will be terrified of you and will do anything you say when not actively avoiding your presence.

BIRTH TO WALKING AGE:

The photo opportunities are limited only by your imagination. If the baby has fallen asleep face down on the floor, scatter empty airline bottles of Jack Daniel's around the body. Or, set the dining room table and use, as a centerpiece, the naked baby fast asleep on a large platter. If you're looking for interesting public reactions, give the baby rubber rats, doggy poop, and giant insects to teethe on before going to the park. Remember, baby faces are simply tiny blank canvases for a world of intriguing makeup possibilities. Heavily pencil-in eyebrows for Joan Crawford: The Very Early Years, utilize a ratty wig and gin bottles for an excellent *Whatever Happened to Baby Jane?* photo op, or simply prop the kid up in a leather chair for a realistic Winston Churchill shot.

TODDLERS TO SPEAKING IN COMPLETE SENTENCES:

At this point in their tiny lives, children are prone to disturbing your pets. This presents the perfect opportunity to teach them that dogs and cats are really savage beasts waiting for an unguarded moment to eat small children. Surreptitiously rub catnip on the little shaver's shoes and feign alarm when you enter the room to see your cats yowling and biting the little one's feet. Sweep the child into your arms and scream with great conviction, "Thank God the dog is outside!"

Chances are it will be years before they ever touch anything with a tail.

THEREAFTER:

Past this point, it is unlikely that they will ever bother you again.

Hey! Your Mom's a Dyke!

S o you're a kid being raised by lesbians. That's not so bad. Some kids are raised by Amish people and they don't even have TV! I know you have TV. How else could mom make you watch all those educational bore-o-rama videos with Marlo Thomas and Shelley Duvall?

You might not realize it but you are very, very lucky. Name one other kid who has two mommies, access to a communal network of wimmin mentors, lots of super-fun uncles, or maybe even an ugly custody battle that could get you on "Oprah"!

Sure, other kids can be really mean and their parents downright hateful, but I'll let you in on a little secret. Even though they may call you a spawn of Satan and refer to your home life as an aberration against God and a tumor in the body of decent America— they are really jealous. Honest! Let's just see how your life stacks up against theirs:

	Heather— Being Raised by Lesbians	Brandy— Being Raised by White Trash	Martha— Being Raised by Fundamentalist Christians
Toys	Dolls, trucks, a Slip 'n Slide, Easy-Bake oven … anything you want, except maybe guns.	Guns, old shopping cart, any of a hundred thousand rusty car parts in the front yard.	Nativity set, the Bible, the garden hose when it's real hot outside, Daddy's penis.
Ability to Get Your Way	Your mom loves you very, very much. So much she probably hardly ever goes to Women's Obsession night at the bar anymore. You'll always get your way.	Brandy is one of 18 or 20 children; she will never get her way because no one remembers her name.	Only selfish, willful children who should be punished with a belt think about themselves.
Chances of Going to Disneyland	Extremely good. Place special emphasis on needing to see the "It's a Small World" exhibit and wanting to commune with the dolphins at Sea World.	Yeahright. Do you know how hard Mom works just to chump-change food stamps for cigarettes, ya little bastard? And you wanna go to Disneyland…	What's Disneyland?

Bent vs. Breeder: The Great Stroller Plan

On the whole, straights are nice people. In fact, my parents are straight and I like them just fine. Essentially, straights in their place (i.e., performing the tedious day-to-day maintenance tasks required to keep our world running smoothly) are quite necessary to the comfort, well-being, and entertainment of the gay populace. It is only when straights become breeders that they begin to tear at the festive fabric that is gay society.

Never mind that a huge chunk of the gay income-tax dollar goes to child welfare, the Aid to Dependent Children fund, and public schools. While these are clearly not gay-related causes, we will continue to subsidize them as a kind of service gratuity for continued existence in North America. Never mind, even, that the most prized gay purchases—cigarettes, dry-cleaning, and liquor—carry outrageous retail taxes that support the public schools.

No, we don't hate breeders for this financial inconvenience. We hate breeders for their strollers.

Perhaps the most annoying accoutrement of the twentieth century, strollers are the bane of homosexual existence. They rival pigeons in their ability to be absolutely everywhere on any formerly pleasant spring day. Considering a mall outing on which one can walk from store to store without tripping over some wheel-assisted five-year-old and his parental entourage? Not in this lifetime. Does the elevator seem to be the most expedient route from point A to point B while running late for an appointment? "Oh, gee, we simply have to cram our screaming four-year-old and her stroller into this car, could you hold the door please?" Strollers are beyond a simple annoyance: They are an impediment to commerce and a very real physical danger—all while being completely unnecessary, as most children are born with feet.

Because I am a lesbian, I am genetically inclined to odd social-betterment methods that worked just fine until the rise of male-dominated Western culture and downfall of female-dominated earth worship. Based on a thorough integration of lesbian-sanctioned ideals, ranging from the sliding-scale payment plan to the Hopi community-based child-raising network, I have formulated a plan for making the world a better place *and* ridding it of strollers:

For every Brittany Wedgewood Lowell born there is undoubtedly a Crystal Amber on government-assisted life support for the prenatally challenged infant. Likewise, for every David Solomon, III, there is indeed a Deewayne Premo one maternity crib over, screaming at the injustice of it all. Rather than impetuously allowing young Britt and David to have a stroller, why not require that half the parental disposable income for these precious gifts from God be dispersed among their less-financially-welcome brothers and sisters, namely Deewayne and Crystal? Essentially, child-bearing would become the grave responsibility it should always have been. Will Dr. and Mrs. Solomon and the Lowells cavalierly bring youngsters into this world knowing that as parents they will be assigned to the Fisher-Price endowment and well-being of the yin to their yang? Subsequently, will Shareka Donika and Brenda Sue Diane continue to bear those children, knowing that they will spend at least eighteen years being hounded by yuppies who now control the purse strings to their child-buying decisions?

Indeed, a workable plan: By distributing the wealth on a one-to-one basis we can reduce the population, guarantee basic necessities for all youngsters, and perpetuate an economy that will dictate children be carried until they can walk.

In keeping with the intrinsically caring and nurturing attitude that has sustained me through all these years, I have once again made life easier and saved the world at the same time.

You're welcome.

• •

Gaydar for
Straight People

····································

I
f you are a straight person working in a company of any size, you have perhaps speculated on the sexuality of a female coworker. Straight people have to speculate because they are not equipped with Gaydar—our genetic gift that is the fruition of aeons of social superiority. Finely honed, Gaydar allows lesbians to put together a damn good softball league from a crowd of any size, and is the reason gay men are able to impetuously form a festive shopping entourage out of seemingly thin air.

Doomed to exist without Gaydar, straights have few options for determining the lesbian in the workplace. Until recently, the only existing lesbian detection method was based on the 1950s interrogation for homosexuals. Devised by former FBI Director J. Edgar Hoover, the original Homosexual Detection questions were used to conclude the sexual status of such flagrant notables as Gertrude Stein, Truman Capote, and Quentin Crisp. Like so many things from the '50s it overstated the obvious while completely avoiding the true aberrational subtleties—namely Roy Cohn and the enormous collection of women's underwear owned by the former director of the FBI.

Granted, someone's sexuality is absolutely none of your business, but, should you be in charge of organizing the company softball team or putting together the next golf outing, lesbian Gaydar can come in quite handy. What follows is a rudimentary Gaydar mechanism specifically designed to determine the lesbian.

QUESTIONS FROM THE '50S TO DETERMINE LESBIANISM, AND WHY THEY DON'T WORK ANYMORE

Does she still live with her mother?
No, no, no. This is used to determine a *gay man.* Geez . . .

Could she be commonly called "handsome" in a way that might suggest tweed and a familiarity with horses?
Are you saying Princess Anne is queer?

Is she a grown woman who shares a house with another grown woman?

In the first half of this century this was relatively conclusive evidence that the woman in question was living with her sister. Today it simply suggests she is living beyond her means.

Is her personal life a mystery?

Well, maybe if you'd shut up for a few minutes and stop nattering on about *your* life, you'd find out about hers. Straight people! They think they've got the market on self-absorption.

QUESTIONS FOR DETERMINING THE '90s LESBIAN, AND WHAT THEY MEAN

Does she have way more disposable income than you?

Without the breeder's financial burden of children—or the single woman's monetary outlay for man-catching enhancements such as breast implants, trendy fashion, fat farms, and *Cosmo* subscriptions—lesbians have incredible discretionary income. The kind of income that allows them to spontaneously spend a few days in Antigua while you're on a last-hope weekend at a Trekkie convention desperately praying for an eligible guy that's not too weird.

Does she refuse to hang out in the employee lunchroom poring over Bride *magazine and gushing about the receptionist's wedding plans?*

The biggest day in a straight woman's life is a satisfying reminder of continued financial freedom for the lesbian. While you are oohing and aahing over $2,000 wedding cakes and exorbitant expenditures in connection with a groom who's barely worthy of oxygen, she is secretly giggling. By refusing to join in, she is kindly saving you the humiliation of hearing her laugh out loud.

Is her personal life a mystery?

Forty years later and straight people are still talking about themselves. Ask to see her pictures from Antigua.

Know Your Gay Signage

Pink or Black Triangle
Homosexual

Labrys
Lesbian

Unicorn
Inexplicable icon of gay
men in the early '80s

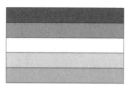

Rainbow Flag
"Proud to Be Gay"

Pink or Gray Triangle
Rudimentary cat's nose

Yellow Triangle
No Passing traffic sign

Axe
Firefighter

Hatchet
Serial killer

My Little Pony
Inexplicable icon of little
girls in the early '80s

Goat
Jamaican restaurant

Skull & Crossbones Flag
"Proud to Be a Pirate"

Confederate Flag
"Proud to Be an Idiot"

What Is Doris?

Cool, calm, confident—gee, the new employee is such a mystery. Is she secretly planning to take over the company and replace the entire staff with eunuchs? Or maybe she's a lesbian, wouldn't that be exciting! Perhaps she'll kill the VP of Marketing with a letter opener—not that that would be such a bad thing, but you should probably ask for your raise right away.

Doris Determinators

Doris usually wears:

A. Clothing designed with such sharp angles even her unoccupied coat is intimidating

B. About three tons of cat fur attached to her sweaters

C. No underpants

I've seen Doris carrying:

A. Confidential files to the copy room

B. A lint brush

C. An ice pick

Doris's signature fragrance seems to be:

A. Chloroform

B. Dial Deodorant Soap

C. Estrogen

I've overheard Doris on the phone saying:

A. "I don't care if he's two weeks from retirement—fire the old bastard!"

B. "Well, she's cute and everything, but the sex just wasn't that good."

C. "How *much* life insurance?"

If I had to cast Doris in a movie, it would be:

A. The lead in *The Leona Helmsley Story*

B. Cagney in *Cagney & Lacey: Trouble at the Dinah Shore*

C. The Barbara Stanwyck role in *Double Indemnity*, only less sympathetic

In her spare time I bet Doris likes to:

A. Geld horses with her bare hands

B. Work on her k.d. lang scrapbook

C. Sit in the bar at the Hyatt holding an unlit cigarette

Doris Index

A. Doris is Joan Crawford on testosterone. She is planning to take over the world one company at a time. Be extremely nice to her and maybe, just maybe, she won't contest your unemployment.

B. Relax! Doris is a garden-variety lesbian. Oh sure, her life's way more fun than yours and her friends are infinitely more fascinating than yours, but other than that she's just like you—only better.

C. Uh-oh. Doris is the kind of crazed female psychopath that you see in the movies all the time. When she's not at home roasting Christian babies or calling the pizza boy/girl so she can open the door naked, she's seducing married people and killing them. Start collecting for the funeral arrangements now—the VP of Marketing is headed for an involuntary retirement.

So You Wanna Be a Straight Girl . . .

If you're a lesbian, occasionally you may want to pass as a straight girl. Not that there are a lot of benefits to this, but sometimes it's fun to see how the other half lives. And this way you don't have to live with oppressed peoples or get a penile implant.

The best place to pretend you are a straight girl is at a new job. Especially one that you don't want to keep for very long. It would be unfortunate to have to get married and bear children just because you've been working at the same place for a couple of years.

Most straight girls are extremely male-identified—both positively and negatively. For example, if the office lech is talking to your breasts, most lesbians will feel perfectly okay in saying, "Stop talking to my tits." Straight girls, however, will see this as either some cosmic affirmation of their desirability or some cosmic affirmation of sexual harassment in the workplace. The former will cause excessive giggling, the latter a million-dollar lawsuit. Either way, straight girls place far too much importance on what the *men* in the office do.

THE LOOK

Remember, *male-identified*. This means combing your hair, daily. It also means wearing clothes that seek and destroy comfort. These are garments designed by gay men to attract heterosexual men. The straight girl is simply the hanger for an inside joke. After a hard day of constructing *prêt-à-porter*, the designers get together for drinks and laugh about it. Real hard.

Single straight girls have a propensity to over-accessorize. Think of those Mexican icons where every possible good luck symbol—Buddha, the Virgin Mary, salt, a four-leaf clover, Jesus, garlic, a horseshoe, the Lucky Blue Dot from the *Enquirer,* an unidentified saint—are all pasted on a single card in hopes that maybe one of them will attract the good luck you so desperately need. That card is a single straight girl. Bracelets, earrings, fake nails, scarves, necklaces, makeup, perfume, hose with designs, false eyelashes, boob jobs—all are trinkets that straight girls paste on themselves in the hope that it might possibly attract a man.

You can easily tell how desperate a woman is by the number of lures she has attached to her costume.

If you're heavy, wear big sweaters over stirrup pants. This will in no way mitigate the fact that you are very fat, but the skinny girls will think this is a trend and begin wearing the same fashion. It will level the playing field and give gay clothing designers a good laugh.

THE ATTITUDE

Initially you must decide what kind of straight girl you are going to be at the office. There are four distinct types to choose from:

Perky:
These women never get fired. They will do silly stupid things like dropping a nail file inside the $25 million copier five minutes before the 5000-page presentation has to go out. Then they will sob in a very perky way. And everyone will forgive them. When they are not vivaciously preparing to weep over some idiotic blunder, they are Mary Richards, only less cynical. They are just too cute to fire. To ensure office productivity, their job descriptions will eventually require them to take the afternoon off to go shopping.

Evil:
This is the office manager kind of girl. The girls that consider the responsibility of ordering office supplies to be the linchpin of Western commerce. If you want to be the evil girl in the office, picture yourself as a *very* bossy Maggie Thatcher. Then be more ruthless. Run a tight ship. Question people about the number of paper clips they've been using. Put disciplinary memos in personnel files. Start vicious rumors. Tattle on slackers. Take over the world.

Underemployed:
Usually this is the receptionist. If she is very good at what she does, she will be indispensable and the office will overlook any number of indiscretions—odd hairstyles, personal calls, a heroin habit—simply to keep her at the front desk. However, she will never get paid what she is worth. Which is about twice as much as the president of the company.

Office Fat Girl:
She will be the one that compulsively organizes office "get-togethers" and the annual blood drive. She tries too hard, and while everyone is nice to her, they usually feel superior. When, and if, she gets married,

the other single girls in the office will be thrown into a snit. If you are portraying the office fat girl, say you are quitting to marry a wealthy partner in a major law firm and then bring in an attractive gay friend as your ruse-fiancé. The other girls will probably choke to death on their own bile.

THOSE EXTRA TOUCHES FOR ADDED REALISM

- Periodically cut out "Cathy" and tape it to your computer.
- Giggle.
- Devote an entire desk drawer to shoes that hurt your feet.
- Buy Hallmark cards on your lunch hour and giggle over them later.
- When you bring your lunch (Lean Cuisine), put it in a trendy shopping bag.
- Flirt outrageously with anything that has a penis, except, ick, *maintenance personnel.*
- Giggle fondly at others' babies and ask to hold them. (Never, *ever* say, "Can I bite him to see what flavor he is?")
- Effusively compliment other women in the office on hideous fashion or hairstyle choices. This is how straight girls reduce competition.
- Feign riveted attention and giggle when a male coworker sits, uninvited, at your lunch table and talks incessantly about how important he is.

DEPROGRAMMING

Wow! Being a straight girl is hard. It's uncomfortable, humiliating, and will probably lead to permanent giggle-lines. When you've had enough of being a straight girl, quit your job and use the following Lesbian Reentry exercises:

1. Locate the nearest straight man—try to avoid your dad—and tell him that you've had enough of internalizing his sexist-patriarchal-oppression crap, and if he doesn't get the fuck out of your face, you'll rip his dick off and slap him with it.

2. Spend an entire week watching Kristy McNichol in reruns of "Family" and "Empty Nest." Play a lot of softball. Drink a lot of lite beer. Flirt outrageously with anything that has ovaries, except, ick, *maintenance personnel.*

3. Hang out with Madonna.

The Phone

There is one foolproof way to differentiate the gay men from the straight men in your office. The phone. Het men will let the phone ring endlessly. Answering the phone is electronic castration for a straight man. It's as though picking up the telephone in an office is the first step down the corporate ladder to a windowless cubical where you have to type your own letters.

Gay men, however, love the phone. I've even seen them pick it up *before* it rings. To a gay man a ringing phone is the ultimate mystery. Who's calling? What do they want? What are they wearing? Even wrong numbers are fascinating to gay men. The phone, quite literally, can be their mother, their best friend, a promotion opportunity or Publisher's Clearing House. Why do you think 900 lines are so popular with gay men? Because it takes the epitome of gay-boy technology and makes it a sex toy. Gay men get shivery just thinking about it.

In the hands of a gay man the phone is the ultimate tool for intrigue and eventual world dominance. They are so intuitive with phones they can get an Ann Landers column out of a two-second office call: "A woman called for Bob, and it wasn't his wife . . . Now why do you think a strange woman would be calling here after five? I think I heard hotel noises in the background and Bob left right after the phone call. I think I'll just Star 69 and see exactly where that phone call came from." Then they'll wait forty minutes and call Bob's house to see if he's home. And finally, they'll call the hotel and ask if there's a room in Bob's name. Mystery solved. If Matlock were queer, he'd never have to leave his office.

In addition to the expert utilization of the vital-information side of the office phone—who won Best Supporting Actress in 1974, how to perform a tracheotomy, what fabrics can't be bleached—the ambitious gay man is capable of manipulating the phone to unlimited promotional opportunities. Simply from being the first to pick up a call and route it to the proper person or take a message, he can determine the weak links, the rivalries, the shaky accounts, the domestic problems and shameful secrets of the entire company. Armed with this information and the ability to access a few simple phone enhancements such as Star 69, speed dial, and automatic redial on other employees' phones, there is *nothing* a gay man can't find out.

When it comes to phone technology, the average MBA-type het, however, is clueless. Due to some archaic instinct concerning spears and mastodons, "fast-track" het men still assume that the only things that are important in life are those things that are hard to kill. The small things—kittens, word processing, kitchen appliances, the phone—are inconsequential, easy-to-manipulate items whose operation is relegated to women and sissies.

This line of thinking is the Darwinism that will bring their own extinction. Straight men will continue to miss answering the important calls and never realize the opportunity this provides for analyzing the power structure. They will remain entirely ignorant of the technology that allows the surreptitious monitoring of inner-office competitors, and eventually they will be passed over for promotions. As the sissy-boy who started out in the fax machine department rises ever higher in the company based on his uncanny knowledge of the "business," the het men will wake up each night sweating over archetypal nightmares of attempting to stab a microchip with an oversized spear. In the office, their names will be mentioned only when an example of some fossilized relic of a bygone era is needed to buttress a point about keeping up with technology. Their days will pass slowly as they sit in a windowless cubicle quietly typing their own letters until retirement . . .

As soon as possible, call the main switchboard after office hours. The man who answers that phone call is the future of American business. Make a special point to connect yourself to his career. And remember it is still perfectly acceptable to use the postal system for sensitive correspondence.

Novel Lesbians

I feel that if we are to put our best foot forward for future generations, we should limit lesbian fiction. I am terrified that three thousand years from now cockroaches will be reading *Curious Wine* and holding book discussions entitled "Lesbians: Simpleminded or Simply Bad Writers?" Or a not-too-future grad student will catalog any of a billion lesbo-mystery novels and receive a doctorate based on her dissertation, "Lesbians in the 21st Century: Were They *All* Detectives?"

We seem to have beaten the hell out of three genres: detective, Southern, and stream-of-consciousness. And not in a good way. I have no idea why lesbians write detective novels; perhaps there's a subculture of lesbo detectives I'm entirely unaware of. And I'm clueless as to why Southern lesbians are always growing up queer-gorgeous-and-damned-funny, except that maybe things are a lot different in the South. Finally, there's that weird stream-of-consciousness novel that James Joyce pioneered, Gertrude Stein exhausted, and intellectual lesbians keep trying to reproduce (we don't reproduce, dammit! we recruit!).

In the interest of making my literary world a better place, I've decided to reveal the basic structure of each of these genres. Then, maybe, we can move on to writing something else.

THE LESBIAN DETECTIVE NOVEL

The Place:
Any town in America

The Plot:
Somebody dies.

The Resolution:
Good triumphs over evil.

Excerpt:

> Burke went back to Joni's apartment. There had to be something that was overlooked. Anything. One thing. Some deus ex machina that would point Burke to the killer. Joni's killer. The warped and

twisted pervert that had tied Joni to that lonely tree in the country. And pitched softball after softball. Until Joni was dead.

Burke was rummaging through Joni's underwear drawer when she saw it. A matchbook. A matchbook from the "Lick'er Bar." A soiled and tattered matchbook. Burke picked up the worn matchbook and opened it with trembling fingers. There it was. A map. A hand-drawn map. A very tiny hand-drawn map. What. Did. It. Mean.?.

THE SOUTHERN LESBIAN NOVEL

The Place:
The kind of tiny rural town where the women eat dirt.

The Plot:
Stunningly attractive Holly GoLesbo is an impetuous madcap that sets the trailer-park town of Squalor, GA, abuzz with her hijinks. It's no wonder that the handsome and wealthy captain of industry, North Caroll Liner, wants this hothouse flower. But it seems that Holly only has eyes for his stable mistress, and the matron at the women's prison, and, well, an itinerant lady truck driver, her mom's best friend, the preacher's wife, and finally a naughty incident with a Girl Scout troop. It's one zany adventure after another as Holly follows her hilarious heart.

The Resolution:
Many, many sequels.

Excerpt:
Holly turned her stunningly beautiful face toward the ravishing Bright Penny Winslow. Her gorgeous brown eyes danced with attractive glee as she spoke. "Bright Penny, I'm afraid the heat, the godawful heat, is about to make me swoon. Why don't we retire to the barn where we will be out of the glare of both the field hands and the sun?"

Bright Penny's breathtaking smile lit up her extra-spectacular features as she whispered, "Why Holly, you have already scandalized the entire town with your activities with my mother. And, now I do declare, you are attempting to seduce me!"

Holly laughed in her very special lovely way and said, "Why

ever not? There are only 13 years between you and your mother and you're both extremely handsome women."

Somewhere, a niggra picked out "Dueling Banjos" on his guitar as Bright Penny and Holly slipped quietly into the barn.

THE AMORPHOUS DEEPER MEANING NOVEL

The Place:
Inside someone's head.

The Plot:
Plot? Now that would just be way too obvious, wouldn't it?

The Resolution:
You finish reading the book.

Excerpt:
> Words like blood flowed from open lips. With translucent angles, they marred the air, landing softly on the carpet, or shattering against the counter until a sharp shard spun off the ice of the occasion and stabbed an errant forehead. "Hey! That hurt," the voice said and the open lips laughed.

Now we're faced with the inevitable question: Well, if you're so smart, what *should* lesbians write about? I would say let's explore some gay-boy-writer territory, but lesbians are genetically incapable of becoming that self-absorbed.

Here's a thought. Write a lesbian humor book. And surprise everyone by actually making it funny.

Gay

Remember when the only reason lesbians were in a movie was because the male director needed a hulking prison matron to keep a bunch of really cute girls in prison? And later it was because he wanted to film some hot sex scenes, like in *The Hunger*? And then when straight women directors wanted to make a "they're people too" point, and they used women like Cher in *Silkwood*? Now it's because the dyke director wants to show a bunch of hulking butchy dykes and one cute girl imprisoned in the Gay Ghetto.

What happened?

The Picture

Personal Best
1982
Patrice Donnelly and Mariel Hemingway
A naive young woman falls prey to the ultimate act of lesbianism—a knee injury, after which, of course, she leaves her girlfriend for a boy.

Desert Hearts
1986
Patricia Charbonneau and Helen Shaver
A divorced woman is pursued by, then pursues, a lesbian relationship, despite the subliminal warning of Patsy Cline singing "Crazy" on the jukebox.

Go Fish
1994
Guinevere Turner and an unwashed cast of thousands
A cute girl falls for a fashion-impaired dyke, making us all feel better if we ever dated someone *really* unattractive or if we *are* really unattractive and hope to ever date a cute girl.

Girl Movies

The Postscript

The Pictorial

Career death for one star, a straight-girl-affirming boob job for the other.

Post-Op Mariel

Both stars granted immediate faculty positions at the JoBeth Williams Made-for-TV-Movie School of Acting.

2:30 p.m. 50 **Gym Class** (CC) Patricia Charbonneau, Helen Shaver. Two PE teachers deal with adolescent hijinks and heartbreak at an exclusive all-girl school. '89 353618 Made for TV

Fifteen minutes of magazine covers, a lifetime of tattoos and piercings.

Director Rose Troche's face weighs well over twenty-five pounds when fully adorned. Above, just one eyebrow's enhancements.

Patsy Cline
and the Impact of Her Hair on Lesbianism Since the 1950s

Patsy, rarely disputed Goddess of Hair in the Lesbian Universe

The Women's PGA Tour Look

Dawn of Lesbianism look still favored by women who are not afraid of laughter, including such notables as former PE teacher Anne Murray, and formerly alive Dinah Shore.

Modified Hair Formation Inspires:

One of the best lesbian careers is grad school. It allows us to constructively use our tedious analytical instinct to spend years preparing a dissertation on fifteen minutes of historical inanity and maybe, eventually, become Camille Paglia.

I can almost guarantee that the fascinating History of Lesbian Hair has not yet been fully researched and can be effortlessly leveraged into grad school acceptance, followed by a book, a full professorship, a write-up in *People* magazine, and finally a coveted guest spot on "Jenny Jones"...

Look of Talent Inspires:

The Tennis Pro Look

Oxymoronic 'do usually accompanied by a V-neck sweater and the intellect of a soap dish. Frequently walked repeatedly from one end of the bar to the other, prompting the less-hair-empowered to shout, **"JESUS CHRIST, WOULD YOU SIT DOWN ALREADY!"**

Hair & Talent Inspires:

Mucho Disposable Income Squandered on Canada's Largest Export (i.e., Lesbian Folk Singers) Inspires:

k.d.

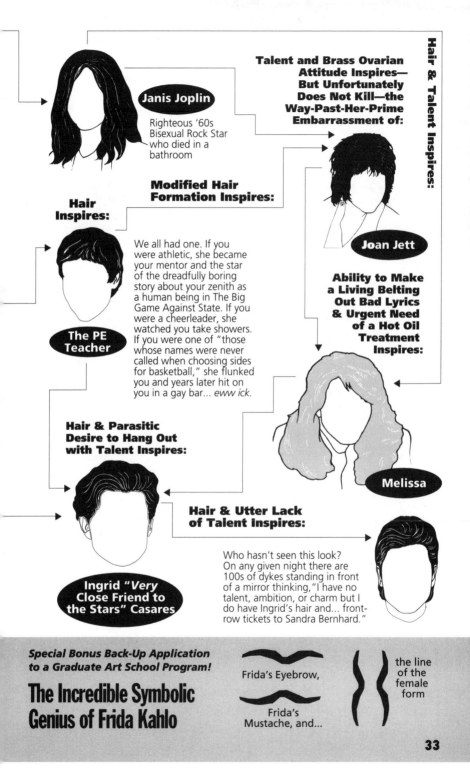

Janis Joplin

Righteous '60s Bisexual Rock Star who died in a bathroom

Talent and Brass Ovarian Attitude Inspires— But Unfortunately Does Not Kill—the Way-Past-Her-Prime Embarrassment of:

Modified Hair Formation Inspires:

Hair Inspires:

We all had one. If you were athletic, she became your mentor and the star of the dreadfully boring story about your zenith as a human being in The Big Game Against State. If you were a cheerleader, she watched you take showers. If you were one of "those whose names were never called when choosing sides for basketball," she flunked you and years later hit on you in a gay bar... *eww ick.*

The PE Teacher

Joan Jett

Ability to Make a Living Belting Out Bad Lyrics & Urgent Need of a Hot Oil Treatment Inspires:

Hair & Parasitic Desire to Hang Out with Talent Inspires:

Hair & Utter Lack of Talent Inspires:

Melissa

Ingrid "*Very* Close Friend to the Stars" Casares

Who hasn't seen this look? On any given night there are 100s of dykes standing in front of a mirror thinking,"I have no talent, ambition, or charm but I do have Ingrid's hair and... front-row tickets to Sandra Bernhard."

Special Bonus Back-Up Application to a Graduate Art School Program!

The Incredible Symbolic Genius of Frida Kahlo

Frida's Eyebrow,

Frida's Mustache, and...

the line of the female form

Special "In the Interest of Science" Literary Revelation:

Not to pick on Ms. Rita Mae Brown, but what is the deal with her eyebrows? A side-by-side chronological comparison of Ms. Brown's dust-jacket pictures reveals an alarming trend:

The Book	The Eyebrows
Rubyfruit Jungle 1973	
Six of One 1978	
Southern Discomfort 1982	
Bingo 1988	
Venus Envy 1993	

The Salman Rushdie Control Eyebrows

2

Liberty

You Do the Math

Numbers, as they say, never lie. So when we attempt to investigate the new, improved homo guestimate of 1 to 2 percent of the population, we see some proven figures of capitalism become, well, highly improbable. Are we really only an average of 1.5 percent of the population? Is it conceivable that a mere 3,730,648 people could be solely supporting the billion-dollar industries of bars, magazines, travel, books, coffeehouses, and direct mail houses that cater exclusively to gays? Are we all sharing an income bracket with David Geffen?

For simplicity—and because I feel wherever I live is the center of the universe—I've chosen Chicago as representative of the United States. In the 312 area code, according to the 1990 U.S. Census, there are 2,783,726 people. 1.5% of that population yields 41,756 homosexuals. In this same area code there are 100 gay bars currently operating. Deduct the national average of 26.5% of the population under 18, 12% over 65, and 13.5% below the poverty line and we have 20,042 gays. Now subtract the national figure of 47.9% of the population that doesn't drink alcohol and we are left with a stunningly thirsty 10,442 gays that have the credentials, inclination, and/or cash to support these bars:

• •

Ongoing Evening Plans for 1.5% of the Population

To maintain the average annual gross of $500,000 for a Chicago homo bar (x 100 bars for $50,000,000),	each and every one of the 10,442 homosexuals must spend	$4,788.35 annually, or $13.11 *every single day* of the year.

I know what you're thinking— "Gee, $92 a week does seem a little high . . ."—but that's only the barest minimum of our fiscal responsibilities. When we factor in all the other gay businesses someone has to support, and then all those endless AIDS benefits, and, finally, we figure the time breakdown of 24 hours in a gay life—we are much more than a mere threat to the fabric of society—we're *super-human:*

24 Busy Hours in a Gay Life

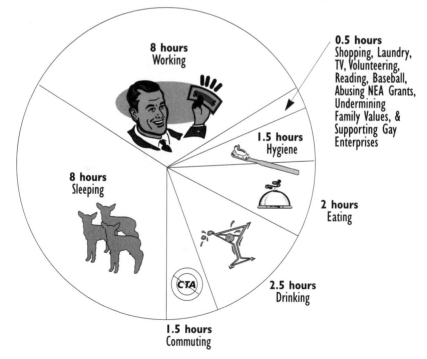

8 hours
Working

0.5 hours
Shopping, Laundry, TV, Volunteering, Reading, Baseball, Abusing NEA Grants, Undermining Family Values, & Supporting Gay Enterprises

1.5 hours
Hygiene

8 hours
Sleeping

2 hours
Eating

2.5 hours
Drinking

1.5 hours
Commuting

Outing

As one might have gathered, working with others' agendas for improving the world is not high on my list of priorities. Indeed, I find many of the radical Gay Rights improvement plans to be especially heinous. Particularly the tactic of Outing. I think it's despicable. Not only because it's a reprehensible and complete violation of one's privacy—but because it's all too often perpetrated on people I'd rather not be associated with.

I'm well aware of the positive gains if a celebrity voluntarily comes out; straight America gets a little bit closer to acknowledging us as normal, younger gays see role models, and a million queers get to say, "I *knew* it."

But a forced Outing invariably comes across as a self-defeating extortion for legitimacy. If we *force* people to come out, what does that say to the straight world?

Aside from the misguided attempts at legitimacy, Outing always seems to concern one of only three groups: people who are dead and thus unavailable for comment; celebrities so consumed with public opinion that Outing them seems inordinately cruel; or people who are so obviously queer that their Outing is akin to announcing that Rush Limbaugh is an idiot.

The Dead:

Basically, they're *dead*. Knowing they *were* queer doesn't mean we can ask them to speak at the next AIDS benefit. And given their current situation, one can't even pretend to have had an inside scoop: "My ex's roommate's lover played pool with Eleanor Roosevelt in Paris, and that Lorena Hickok was all over her. I *knew* she was queer."

The Celebrity:

This is just plain mean. We're taunting a group whose only talent is photographing well and whose life's passion is to be liked, really, really liked. A simple people who have to be directed in speaking dialogue they haven't written. If it weren't for the advent of the camera, they would probably be not terribly intelligent receptionists or flight attendants.

And honestly, do we really *want* to be associated with Drew Barrymore?

The Obvious:

"What? k.d. lang is queer?" Now who didn't know this? Blind people in rural Iowa?

Elton John, Liberace, and Martina Navratilova were all publicly Outed at one time or another. How the world continued to spin after these revelations is a fitting tribute to the durable construction of the universe.

As with any announcement concerning a minority, the only people who truly think it's interesting are members of that minority.

Here's a lesson I've learned about the importance of homosexuality in the grand scheme of things; Does your mom read *People* magazine? Mine neither. But I figured since the TV is occasionally turned on, she must have *some* kind of clue as to who's in and who's out. So, I tell my mother, "Well, you know Melissa Etheridge is gay . . ." And she says, "Isn't she the one that got all of you girls to start smoking? I never liked any of your high school friends . . ."

For many people, the word "outing" implies something entirely different than revealing one's homosexuality. Why rain on my mom's picnic?

•••••••••••••••••••••••••

The Name Game

As part of a subculture that takes nomenclature *extremely* seriously, I found myself rather embarrassed recently. I could not recall the Politically Correct word for "midget." I scoured fifteen years of lesbo life for the positive descriptor of midget. I obsessed. I drank. I smoked cigarettes. I bought a fur coat. I did every un-PC stress-reducing thing I could while trying to come up with that word. What the hell is positive for midget—homunculus? personette? leprechaun? dwarf?

Other than selfishly wishing a midget were always seated in front of me at the movies, I'm deeply ashamed to admit I had never given them a second thought.

Finally I broke down and asked a lesbian friend what the preferred name was for, ummm, like uhhh, well, people who probably had to utilize both Chicago phonebooks when they drove. She said, "Little People." Little People? They *want* to be called Little People?! I was stunned. I pictured the backlash of Little People empowering themselves with the hurtful labels: "We're midgets! We're proud! We'll keep it short and say it out loud!"; then organizing a Little People Day at Disney World where they could rush the height checkpoint on the way to the Matterhorn and vocally denounce Snow White; and eventually making those same labels a proud part of their culture: "I'm having a small bunch of dwarves over for brunch on Sunday, can you come?"

It's just gone too far. We've reached the point where *even a lesbian* can't keep track of it all. And while we're at it, why *are* lesbians the self-appointed name-game guardians of minorities? Why are *we* expected to remember and promote the preferred label—no matter how silly—of every single special interest group?

Perhaps lesbians play the name game because of the Michigan Womyn's Festival, our annual big lesbo powwow. As we can't make a group decision on anything, it's only appropriate that the most pertinent achievement to come out of Michigan is twenty-four different ways to spell woman.

And once you've accomplished that, the rest of the world is simply one big grammatical challenge.

This phrase	replaces this word(s)	because
Differently Abled	retarded, handicapped, or challenged	differently-abled people are much more skilled than mono-abled people in many areas, including: getting the lids off jars (wheelchair-assisted persons), count toothpicks (Rain Man), passing legislation, and always getting the good parking spaces.
Definitely Tabled	ultimate end to any legislation concerning homosexual rights	we're tired of saying "defeated."
Differently Cabled	cable pirate(s)	"pirate" belittles buccaneers, and "cable pirate" associates the illustrious history of the noble buccaneer with the petty thievery of HBO and Showtime.
Distantly Bay Bold	former Feather Heather color selection in the Lands' End catalog	the creative director wanted something "less whimsical, more masculine . . ."
Securely Cradled	trailer court	maybe if we change the name to something positive, the tornadoes won't know where to touch down.
Feloniously Enabled	convicts	prison isn't necessarily a negative experience, and by putting the emphasis on the positive "enabling" aspects of incarceration—warmth, food, twenty-four-hour companionship—perhaps we'll begin to see it as just a nice place to keep scary people.
Defiantly Garbled	angry, drunken, harelip	actually, this doesn't replace anything, but geez, have you ever heard the Defiantly Garbled before? There *needs* to be a term for it . . .

Scientific A-*mary*-ca

I am entranced with the concept of Darwinism. It makes me happy to know that the human race is slowly being winnowed to the best and the brightest. The best part of Darwinism is that it doesn't affect queers in the least. Our appearance is simply a benefit-blip on the face of evolution.

Thousands and thousands of years from now, gays will be enjoying the genetic refinements of nature's very selective breeding. I picture us sipping cocktails, *rive gauche*, while casually watching the straight people scurry to attend to our every need. I also predict the end of the "Don't" sections of fashion magazines accompanied by the rise of a fully toothed people who have no words for "trailer court."

Oh well, that's neither here nor there. The questions before us are: Who has Darwinism most obviously targeted? How will it happen? And how long do we have to wait?

THE FAR RIGHT NRA SEGMENT

How Is It Going to Happen?
You may wonder why nature wasted thumbs on these people. I'll tell you. Once upon a time we needed them to commit violent acts on large animals so we could all eat. Now the addition of a thumb leads primarily to their offspring accidentally shooting themselves with the loaded guns they keep in their homes. Why? Because they are no longer necessary, and the laws of Darwinism have dictated that *they are so expendable that their genetic line should not continue.* That's why.

How Long Do We Have to Wait?
In two hundred years the NRA will be reduced to a dusty handgun exhibit in the "Cause and Effect: The End of Idiots in America" section of local museums. Yes, it's a long time to wait, but it will happen.

THE INNER CITY

How Is It Going to Happen?
A number of forces seem to have ganged up on the inner city. Internal genocide, external genocide, and life without hope of parole. But perhaps the most interesting development is the alarming trend of children falling out of the windows in high-rise housing projects. One

might conclude that there is direct correlation between these deaths and a lack of parental supervision, or that it's the cities' fault for not reinstalling window guards as soon as they are torn out by the residents. Nope. It's not the parents' fault, it's not the cities' fault—yes, the laws of gravity are now picking off the poor.

How Long Do We Have to Wait?
If the physical laws continue to influence the evolutionary decline of the inner city, we can expect escalating incidents of gravitational, convection, and wave/particle deaths. Utilizing the Theory of Localized Entropy, we can predict that the icky parts of every city will be sucked into a black hole at approximately 12:00 p.m. EST sometime during the third millennium.

THIRD WORLD INHABITANTS

How Is It Going to Happen?
Oh sure, without the wretched refuse from other teeming shores we'll be completely deprived of domestic help and cab drivers, but it can't be avoided. You're looking at people who consider dirt and bugs to be the bottom of the food pyramid. Add the ubiquitous civil wars and the fact that many are attempting to develop an agrarian culture *in the desert*, and it's unlikely that they will continue to be a big part of the big picture.

How Long Do We Have to Wait?
Second to securing food, the Third World considers having babies to be a viable career path. Thus the Third World creates its own, rather faulty, biosphere. If we cut the two supply hoses of pro-procreative Catholicism and emergency aid, the population will level out to four well-fed people in a matter of decades.

A SUPPOSITION

Breast and ovarian cancer are two of the leading causes of death among lesbians. Studies have shown that these cancers strike lesbians more frequently because we don't have children. Could this be nature's way of telling us that we are the chosen refinement, and expected to have and raise the best generation?

Probably.

Homo Rage

'm intrigued with the whole minority-rage defense for criminals. On the queer side, I know that it explains a lot of previously unexplainable social slights. Aside from the really creepy acts of homo rage—the interior of Trump Tower and snotty flight attendants—I'm certain most straights have unwittingly been victims of an edgy queer acting out long-smoldering aggression.

DETERMINING HOMO RAGE

If you've ever been a victim of	it's probably because
a severely bad haircut	you undertipped last time—Renaldo is an artiste and does not like this treatment.
being snubbed by the mâitre d' and given the table next to the toilets	you have a severely bad haircut.
smirking	you look ridiculous sitting next to the toilets in that severely bad haircut.
retail rudeness	you've offended the employees by appearing in their chichi boutique when your haircut so obviously indicates a complete lack of taste.
audible tittering over your fashion sense	you're wearing something from the Jaclyn Smith collection.
eye rolling	you've announced that Newt Gingrich has some solid ideas for this country.
extreme sullenness from the wait-staff	you asked for water.
ugly floral arrangements	you are the philistine that requested baby's breath in the arrangement.
sloppy UPS delivery	you are not femme enough for the driver—next time try a little perfume, okay hun? And do something about that hair . . .

There is a simple reason queers belittle straight people: because we can. As queers are a large percentage of the service workforce, straights are continuously in contact with us while rarely bothering to acknowledge our existence. We are in a prime position to extract revenge—a revenge that makes the following common statement all the more tragic: "I can't see that gays are a large enough group to demand explicit human rights. *I* certainly don't know any gay people . . ." With this attitude your hairstyle will always be a source of amusement.

Be grateful we don't run the post office.

If you want to be consistently assured of top-flight service in any capacity, surgically alter yourself to pass as Barbra Streisand. No gay, anywhere—even if they *hate* Barbra Streisand—will treat you rudely. Ms. Streisand is a kind of celestial icon radiating over Planet Queer, and being rude to her is grounds for banishment to Utah for a lifetime with the Mormons. It's just not worth it.

Homo Rage: A Case Study

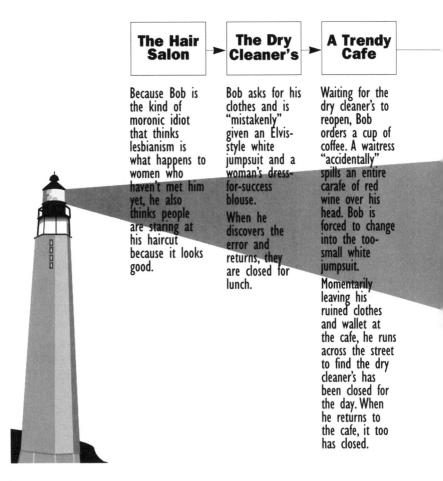

The Hair Salon	→	The Dry Cleaner's	→	A Trendy Cafe

The Hair Salon

Because Bob is the kind of moronic idiot that thinks lesbianism is what happens to women who haven't met him yet, he also thinks people are staring at his haircut because it looks good.

The Dry Cleaner's

Bob asks for his clothes and is "mistakenly" given an Elvis-style white jumpsuit and a woman's dress-for-success blouse.

When he discovers the error and returns, they are closed for lunch.

A Trendy Cafe

Waiting for the dry cleaner's to reopen, Bob orders a cup of coffee. A waitress "accidentally" spills an entire carafe of red wine over his head. Bob is forced to change into the too-small white jumpsuit.

Momentarily leaving his ruined clothes and wallet at the cafe, he runs across the street to find the dry cleaner's has been closed for the day. When he returns to the cafe, it too has closed.

Gay hairstylists serve as a kind of vanguard for the rest of the queer community. By giving a bad haircut they send a signal: "This person is a bigoted idiot, treat them accordingly."

For example, just this morning Bob told his rather attractive hairstylist, Leslie, that she wasn't really a lesbian, she just hadn't found the right man yet (wink-wink). She responded by giving him the Big Stupid Jerk cut.

OOOHHHWAA! OOOHHHWAA! Yes, that's Bob's hair now giving out an I'm-an-asshole alert to every queer he meets. Let's just see how Bob's day progresses, shall we?

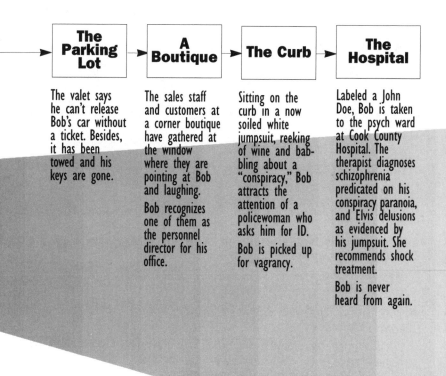

The Parking Lot	A Boutique	The Curb	The Hospital
The valet says he can't release Bob's car without a ticket. Besides, it has been towed and his keys are gone.	The sales staff and customers at a corner boutique have gathered at the window where they are pointing at Bob and laughing. Bob recognizes one of them as the personnel director for his office.	Sitting on the curb in a now soiled white jumpsuit, reeking of wine and babbling about a "conspiracy," Bob attracts the attention of a policewoman who asks him for ID. Bob is picked up for vagrancy.	Labeled a John Doe, Bob is taken to the psych ward at Cook County Hospital. The therapist diagnoses schizophrenia predicated on his conspiracy paranoia, and Elvis delusions as evidenced by his jumpsuit. She recommends shock treatment. Bob is never heard from again.

Ask the Experts

Nobody knows more about you and your lifestyle than God. And nobody knows more about God than the Far Right. Because God is unlisted, the Far Right has become the self-appointed link between the Big White Guy and What He Wants Us to Do.

So, the next time you're contemplating your sad, pathetic homosexual lifestyle, filled with tortured days of minding your own business and paying taxes, you might want to ask the Far Right a few questions about your sickness, your fundamental evilness, and the possibility that you will single-handedly cause the end of the world.

And certainly, who better to judge your life than a bunch of white guys whose only brush with sexuality is conclusive allegations of sexual harassment or that incident with a twelve-year-old boy in the backseat of a Buick? Whoops! Did I say that? Jesus Christ, I'm sorry . . .

• •

If they're so abhorrent, why does God make gays?
God doesn't make gays—gays make God puke. Satan, domineering mothers, and absent fathers make gays.

Oh. Is that why highly respected Far Right Spokeswoman Phyllis Schlafly has a gay son?
Next question.

If gays were granted full civil rights, what's the worst-case scenario?
Decent Americans would be exposed to homo teachers, homo soldiers, and the—*make God puke*—homo agenda.

Oh. So America would emulate the foundation for Western civilization—ancient Greece?
Next question.

Why do you hate me so much?

We don't hate you, we hate the putrid demon that's living in your soul. And if we have to dismantle your body to evict that demon, well then, so be it.

Do you ever wonder why there is an inverse relation between your supporters and dental hygiene?

Fluoridated water is a known Communist plot, and any real American should be proud not to have teeth.

Is there anything worse than being gay?

We would say being the Antichrist, but we think you might be the Antichrist, so we would have to say being Hillary Clinton.

• •

Far Right Experts Trading Cards!

Collect 'em! Trade 'em! Clamp 'em real tight to your bike spokes for realistic whining noise!

Clarence Thomas

Black like . . . well, Mandingo.

Most Electrifying Moment:
Seated comfortably in his chair, denouncing his Senate hearing as an "electronic lynching" while "uppity" Anita Hill twisted in the wind

Odd Contradiction:
Vocally anti-entitlement, yet strangely silent when Bush represented him, with his beginner judicial experience, as "the best person for the job"

"Odd Contradiction" Gameplan:
Supreme Court Appointment

If Associated with Pro Sports He Would Be:
Mike Tyson or maybe a kinder, gentler O. J. Simpson.

Card Value:
11 = Free Adult Video

Often confused with Phil Gramm—another Senate fossil who wears his glasses too tight.

Most Electrifying Moment:
Saying the words "Long Dong Silver" and "pubic hair" in front of God and everyone on national TV

Odd Contradiction:
Staunchly supports both the anti-Choice movement and the tobacco industry

Possible "Odd Contradiction" Gameplan:
Each unborn child represents a possible tobacco user—a consumer base that could keep Helms in the Senate long after more than just his brain has died

If Associated with Pro Sports He Would Be:
Marge Shott

Card Value:
10 + 5 Raleigh Coupons = An Orphan

Jesse Helms

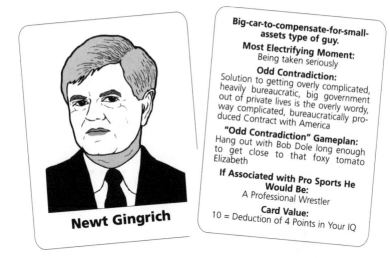

Newt Gingrich

Big-car-to-compensate-for-small-assets type of guy.

Most Electrifying Moment:
Being taken seriously

Odd Contradiction:
Solution to getting overly complicated, heavily bureaucratic, big government out of private lives is the overly wordy, way complicated, bureaucratically produced Contract with America

"Odd Contradiction" Gameplan:
Hang out with Bob Dole long enough to get close to that foxy tomato Elizabeth

If Associated with Pro Sports He Would Be:
A Professional Wrestler

Card Value:
10 = Deduction of 4 Points in Your IQ

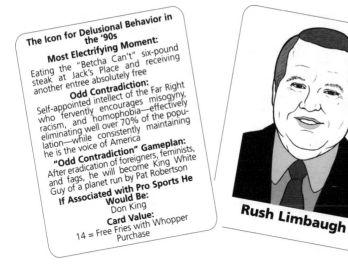

The Icon for Delusional Behavior in the '90s

Most Electrifying Moment:
Eating the "Betcha Can't" six-pound steak at Jack's Place and receiving another entree absolutely free

Odd Contradiction:
Self-appointed intellect of the Far Right who fervently encourages misogyny, racism, and homophobia—effectively eliminating well over 70% of the population—while consistently maintaining he is the voice of America

"Odd Contradiction" Gameplan:
After eradication of foreigners, feminists, and fags, he will become King White Guy of a planet run by Pat Robertson

If Associated with Pro Sports He Would Be:
Don King

Card Value:
14 = Free Fries with Whopper Purchase

Rush Limbaugh

To prove that the Far Right speaks for just as many Americans as the liberals, we've included, on our Ask the Experts Panel: a disgusting fat slob, a suspected black man, a crotchety senior citizen, and a guy with far too few thoughts for such an enormous head.

Equal Time

And while we're on the subject of the insentient—what do you think the dead liberal heroes are doing? That's right, spinning in their graves!

Included here is a fun representation of an All-Star graveyard. Simply paste front and back pieces together, stab them with a pencil, and you've got a liberal top that will spin and spin and spin—just as they're probably doing right now!

The Reverend Dr. Martin Luther King, Jr.: What happens to a dream ◯ deferred? It explodes.

Arguably a product of artificial insemination, definitely a proponent of love and acceptance, this lifelong bachelor is now being ◯ slandered as a key architect of the hatred, fear, and ignorance tactics of the Far Right and their Family Values. Jesus wept.

It's whispered by the locals that one can feel quite a nice breeze when standing ◯ on top of Ms. Roosevelt's grave.

Soon to be annexed to an entirely different part of the cemetery:

Though still alive by the barest standards of brain activity, upon his death Senator ◯ Thurmond may well rotate on a spit in a place entirely too warm for comfort.

The Voice of the Right

Occasionally I listen to Christian radio. I think that maybe, if the Rapture ever comes, the one thing that will determine my being lifted to heaven or staying here for aeons of pestilence is the off-chance that I might be listening to God radio. I don't believe I'll ever win the lottery either—but sometimes I buy a ticket. Just in case.

God radio is truly the last intellectual frontier. There is no idea that is too far Left, too far Right, or too fourth dimensional not to merit a discussion on God radio. They say we lead a deviant lifestyle, but frankly, if even a small group of queers equated handling rattlesnakes with divinity, I'd make an effort to remove myself from the overall movement.

One of the benefits of perusing God radio is finding out the purge-the-queers tactics before they become a Senate committee hearing. Essentially they'd like to kill us, but on a global scale that's somewhat impractical. So they propose any number of laws—forcibly curing us, forcibly tattooing us, and forced penal colonies. And the proposed mandatory sentence for violating any of these laws? Death.

I've been trying to figure out the Far Right Christian argument against gays for years. One would like to assume such virulent hatred of a group is based on something verifiable. Like, oh say, our leaders are regularly jailed for financial improprieties, or we support our causes by scamming old people for money, or we bomb medical clinics, or even that we have a history borrowing lawn tools and never returning them. Anything.

The three "God hates faggots" arguments, as best as I can follow, are:

The Bible says it's wrong.

Oh, and what an excellent literal guidebook for life in the twenty-first century! Along with the abomination of a man-lying-with-a-man stricture, here's some more You'll-Go-Straight-to-Hell-Don'ts from the good book: 1. Never plow with both an ox and a mule (Deuteronomy 22:10), 2. Don't ever wear a cotton shirt with that wool suit (Deuteronomy 22:11), and 3. Say goodbye to football forever because handling pigskin is wrong, wrong, wrong (Leviticus 11:7–8). Not that it's all negative; here's a helpful hint found in Leviticus: If you've got leprosy in your house and nothing seems to work, have a priest kill a bird in a clay pot over running water. Now, dip a live bird, cedarwood, scarlet, and hyssop into the dead bird's blood and sprinkle your house seven times. (This also works with clothing and actual lepers.)

We are sexual predators and/or we recruit because we can't reproduce.

And there's nothing any of us want more than a relationship with a twelve-year-old Christian kid who has a home-schooling education. But when it comes down to using children to perpetuate your own twisted ends, between the story of Lot and the Catholic hierarchy I think the Christians might need to devote some extensive work on transference issues . . .

We choose to be gay.

No, one *chooses* to be a good person, just as one chooses the best shade of lipstick to set off one's henna rinse. Some of us are born gay. In much the same way the Far Christian Right is *born* agreeable, and *chooses* to be bigoted, hateful, and wear polyester clothing.

There. I think I've cleared that up sufficiently. Now the Christian Right is perfectly free to get on with misconstruing the "Judge Not . . ." and "Love Your Neighbor . . ." parts of the Bible. And while they're at it they might want to consider rereading Revelation, because when it comes to the Rapture, it sounds as if the aeons of pestilence left on the earth *just might be them.*

Another Gay for Dorothy

Someone—I don't remember who, I only remember it should have been me—once proposed that gays form their own religion so that we could bypass the struggle for basic human rights by protesting injustices on the grounds of religious discrimination. A darn good idea. As it is, there is already a very strong Cult of Dorothy existing in the gay community that eerily parallels the Evangelical Christian movement. Note that certain glassy-eyed zeal in telling and retelling the story, the literal belief in a very old—very fantastical—tale, the overwhelming joy in worshipping the icon, the silly songs, the overproduced musicals, and the gaudy T-shirts—all of the components of Evangelical Christianity are firmly in place in the Cult of Dorothy.

In fact, when it comes to establishing a historical being as a factual icon of religious proportions, gays have it all with one big difference—we've got pictures. With scant effort, we could leverage ourselves into a bona fide religion.

Let's begin. Contrast the oddly similar promises of a final reward for true believers: Evangelicals picture heaven as a predominantly white suburb with no crime or carbon dating. In comparison, what could be closer to gay nirvana than the tastefully decorated Emerald City with its emphasis on retailers devoted to appearance and the everyday-is-a-parade atmosphere?

Closer examination reveals even more startling similarities between the Cult of Dorothy and Evangelical Christians, particularly in the code words used to define like persons:

The Evangelical	The Dorothy
Do you know Jesus?	Do you know Dorothy?
Is she a friend of Jesus?	Is she a friend of Dorothy's?
Trust Jesus	Surrender Dorothy
There's no place like heaven	There's no place like home
The peace that passeth all understanding	Poppies, beautiful poppies

More Oddly Parallel Differences

In addition to the promise of heaven, Dorothys and Evangelicals split hairs on a few theological fine points:

The Basic Setup

Evangelical Christians are patriarchal, with violent sub-icons such as the guy that killed all those people with a donkey's jawbone, Satan, and the Right to Lifers.

Dorothys are matriarchal, with nonviolent sub-icons such as Maria Callas, Old Movie Stars, and Barbra Streisand.

Public Policies Concerning the Disabled:

The undisputed champion in assisting the most severely disabled, Jesus raised the dead.

Dorothy nobly aided the Scarecrow and the Tin Man in their quest for missing organs, and she played a key role in comforting and restuffing the Scarecrow when his disabilities were cruelly exploited by the Wicked Witch's flying monkeys.

Public Policies Concerning Evil:

Jesus refused a number of offers by the devil, including valuable real estate holdings and his own immortality in exchange for his soul.

Dorothy defeated evil by symbolic cleansing, literally baptizing the Wicked Witch out of existence.

Public Policies Concerning Tolerance:

Perhaps tolerance's greatest spokesperson, Jesus is credited with developing the Golden Rule and numerous "Let ye without sin cast the first stone/Judge not, lest you be judged" types of adages.

Despite the Lion's incessant blathering, Dorothy continued to respect his needs and assisted him in seeking help to correct his fatal character flaw. She also tirelessly worked to develop relationships with beings not even of her own species.

Message for a New Millennium:

"Do unto others as you would have done unto you."

Jesus Christ of Nazareth

"Follow the yellow brick road."

Dorothy Gale of Kansas

The groundwork has been set. If we do establish ourselves as the Cult of Dorothy, we can *really* recruit, legally manipulate money from old people, and spend huge amounts of tax dollars toward the fight to have pictures of Dorothy in the post office.

Of course, if the whole Dorothy thing sounds like just too much work, we can always campaign to have homosexuality reclassified as a disease/disability. Naturally, this will set the movement back a couple of decades—but think of those parking spaces. And who doesn't want those great big bathroom stalls in all the bars?

3

· · · · · · · · · · · · · · · · ·

The Pursuit
of Happiness

The Birth of Marie DuGuerre

As names go, Mary Dugger is ambiguous. I hear Mary Dugger and I picture a cafeteria lady with a hair net. But friends have said, "It's not a negative name, Mary, it's a challenge." Then they cheer me up with qualifiers like,

"𝕿𝖍𝖊 𝖂𝖗𝖊𝖈𝖐 𝖔𝖋 𝖙𝖍𝖊 𝕸𝖆𝖗𝖞 𝕯𝖚𝖌𝖌𝖊𝖗.

Mary Dugger reporting live from Washington.

INMATE: MARY DUGGER.

```
Mary Dugger, there are four hours I can't account
for on a dirt road in Indiana."
```

It's like Vanna White, a name rife with possibilities. But I don't want a name that incorporates the gray space between glamour and a hair net.

I moved to Chicago because I thought the humidity would make my hair look thicker. So I arrived, presented myself as a devil-may-care madcap with abundantly thick hair, and—Chicago turned a cold broad shoulder.

Crushed, I did what I always do when faced with rejection; I avoided self-examination and plotted revenge. I developed a glamorous, yet glamorously disdainful, alter ego with the terrific name of Marie DuGuerre, and proceeded to work through my bitterness by parceling it out to everybody else. Marie began writing for a very happenin' Chicago queer rag, *gab*, where she pissed a lot of people off. As Marie would say, *"Pardonnez-moi? Like I care?"*

The best alter ego I know belonged to my friend Keith. Her name was Mrs. Douglas. She showed up to hostess his parties—including the highly awaited annual Violent Croquet Soirée—beautifully wrap all his Xmas gifts, pen wonderfully warm thank-you notes, and bake fabulous desserts. Mrs. Douglas was Martha Stewart well before Martha Stewart was Martha Stewart. Tragically, Mrs. Douglas was killed when she slipped on some meringue in the kitchen and hit her head on the oven. Keith had to bury her in his backyard.

Marie DuGuerre is sort of the antithesis of Mrs. Douglas. Marie writes bad checks to charity, serves her friend Mary Deb's cheesecake on Chinet and says she made it herself, takes credit for every funny thing she's ever repeated, and is the social equivalent of Camille Paglia, only more convinced of her intellectual superiority. I figured Chicago deserved somebody like Marie.

What follows is Marie DuGuerre: The Chicago Years. She looks for love, she dispenses advice, she tirelessly makes fun, she's so self-absorbed she has her own gravitational pull. Essentially, she is less than a successful lesbian at most any social gathering.

Be forewarned that Marie sometimes writes in the first person, occasionally in third, and frequently it makes no sense at all. But as Marie might say, "Live with it."

●●●●●●●●●●●●●●●●●●●●●●●●●●●●●●●●●●

Dark Secrets

If you've paid attention up to this point, you may have noticed that I have a fascination with hair, particularly eyebrows. I think they are potentially the most attractive feature on the human body. Keanu Reeves in *Speed* had the world's perfect eyebrows. Symmetrical, insouciantly arched, exactly the right tapering quality. My friend Sue, though I've never told her this, has the most perfect eyebrows I've ever seen in real life. These are eyebrows you could gaze at forever. The kind of eyebrows you would be proud to be seen with. I'm always afraid that she'll catch me swooning over her eyebrows and think she has something on her forehead. So I surreptitiously stare, making everybody else think she has something on her forehead.

This is a bizarre, rather pathetic, part of myself that can be traced back to childhood trauma. By sharing this I hope to overcome these particular emotional scars and move on to analyzing other bizarre, rather pathetic, parts of myself.

As a wee nipper I had the kind of eyebrows that made my parents' friends say, "She has such a pretty smile." Thick, dark, foreboding eyebrows. Not the unibrow (thank God) but that odd, my-but-Marie-has-a-*lot*-of-eyebrow-for-a-homo-sapien look.

As a young girl I wore long bangs and teachers were always calling out, *in front of the entire class*, "Marie, please get that hair out of your eyes," activating the kind of stop-and-stare classroom PR that scars one for all eternity.

When I was a teenager the height of girl-teen fashion was Farrah Fawcett. She had eyebrows that were a little under one hair wide. One day I threw rationality to the wind and decided to pluck my eye brows. Four hours later I was in intense pain and had succeeded in partially reducing one brow to the thickness of a kitten's tail. I have never been slave to fashion since.

Eventually Brooke Shields made it big, and for the first time in my life I was a fashion barometer. But it was too late, the scars were already there. To this day when I see my old friend Sara, who so over-plucked her brows that she has to manufacture new ones every morning with an eye pencil, I secretly gloat.

Thanks for letting me share.

• •

The Eyebrow Calculator

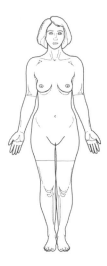

Perhaps the only thing between you and a movie career is your eyebrow shape and color. Marie, too, thought this might be a possibility. So she developed the Eyebrow Calculator—a revolutionary idea in beauty, and your key to stardom. In fact . . . *What? Oh! Whoops! Gotta run, Steven Spielberg's on the phone . . .*

Instructions

Cut out individual brow sets—DO NOT mix and match—and place on facial outline.

When you have chosen the brows you feel are most attractive, use the office copier to enlarge approximately 600%.

Copy several times and employ hair-shade-comparable crayons to color in your new brows.

Tape to your face. Ask around the office as to which is most flattering. Apply for unemployment.

Use this time off to make your new eyebrows, move to California, and start auditioning.

The Foster

The Joan

The Maria Von Trapp

The Pretty Baby

Despite a complete eyebrow deficit, Whoopi Goldberg is one of the most highly paid women in Hollywood.

Men Only

The only thing that ever makes me wish I was born a gay man is the all-boy venues. It's not that I really want to get in, but once that line has been drawn I feel I'm missing out on something. And according to the ads that feature pictures of huge sundecks and beautiful men, I am. You never see that in a Michigan Womyn's Festival brochure. They always make it look exactly like what it is—tedious.

While I have endlessly pressed my boy friends to take me to all-boy places, only one friend has ever asked me to take him to Michigan. He is an actor, and in drag he is a very convincing, very big, Gertrude Stein. His sole reason for attending is his certainty that he will be questioned about his gender. He has conceived a four-hankie monologue about an optimistic girlhood eroded by a cold world of ridicule, and a forlorn adult shattered by the questioning of an outward appearance that belies the warm, compassionate, gentle woman inside. He maintains it will be his finest performance. I maintain they'll never question his masculinity because there'll be at least a hundred women there that can beat him at arm-wrestling.

Once I stayed at an all-male hotel in Manhattan. It was fabulous. Every time I left my room an entire hallway of doors would open a teeny bit and heads would appear. As soon as they saw a woman, the heads would disappear and the doors would slam shut. The power was exhilarating. I spent hours roaming the halls and reveling in the *slam, slam, slam* that announced my arrival. All too soon the boy friend who'd booked the room was called by the concierge, who requested that the "tuna" staying with him find other accommodations. I retaliated by hanging a tampon from every doorknob in the building. My friend can no longer stay at this hotel. But hey, with all that door slamming, who wants to?

Essentially it all comes down to this: I come back from Michigan and tell my boy friends, "It rained nonstop, many women refused to ever wear clothes even though the vegetarian-enforced buffet table was at pubic-hair level, a woman with a beard yelled at me about wearing fur, there were more rules than the long version of Monopoly, and I was forced to participate in a Kumbayah sing-along every night." My boy friends come back from the clubhouse and tell me, "I met the guy that made the movie in the downstairs screening room, then I had hot sex with a Broadway lyricist who wants to look at my songs, Bette Midler dropped by to sing a couple of numbers in the upstairs dance complex, and, oh, I won a car in the raffle, but it was boring, Marie. Honest."

Yeah, right.

● ●

Marie DuGuerre,

a.k.a.

gwf

looking for

Love.

MEN

HOT DADDY has rim chair. Me top you under.

SPERM DONOR WANTED: Are you 7" cut+, nice mushroom head, shoots loads of cum, HIV-, 25–35, 5'9", clean & attractive, have nice shaped feet & like to have them licked, not overweight, can cum more than once? Call me!

THROAT DEPTH inspections: 4 appt send Polaroid/frontal and phone.

ewwww ick

Because women sharing these interests call it "Getting ready for work."

HAIRCUTTING, bodyshaving turn you on? Meet men sharing these interests.

?

(Excluding travel.)

GWM INCARCERATED, 5'9", 170#, honest, sincere, intelligent, mature with a good sense of humor. Open to all possibilities at present. All replies welcome.

, barbecuing in Hell,

GWM 47 Y/O, 5'9", 170#, Fundamentalist Christian who enjoys outdoors, cooking, and being home. ISO GBM or GHM to share and spend time with. Write.

Once upon a time, queers met by going to disreputable dives, tentatively talking to likely suspects and taking their chances. Oh, sure, you might have been arrested, and there was always the chance you'd be beaten to death by sailors or imprisoned in a mental home—but on the plus side, you never had to make a dating decision based on a personal ad that featured naked self-disclosure...

WOMEN

GWF, 35, CARING, 5'5", 185#, br hr/eyes, loves long walks, movies and long winter nights to share with someone special. Are you the one?

To where? The 7/11 for donuts?

GWF, PROFESSIONAL, seeking independent same/financially stable, career oriented/successful. Enjoy fine dining, opera, international travel. No fats, fetishes, smokers, drugs, drinkers.

Essentially, no obsessive behavior that might eclipse that oh-so-healthy devotion to money.

ATHLETIC GWF, TRIATHLETE. Enjoy long runs, biking, swimming, volleyball and attending pro sports. ISO fit GWF not into games, old lovers or bar scene.

Oh, and team sports don't count?

I HOLD YOU AGAINST all odds, the love we have is perfect/pure, then I awake and I am alone. I will search for you, please walk out of my dream.

And what if I did and then I turned into your mom and all of a sudden you were naked in this long hallway trying to find the math test you hadn't studied for—Then you'd be sorry...

ACTUAL ADS! ONLY SLIGHTLY ALTERED TO AVOID A LAWSUIT

Putting the Data Back into Dating

I am much older than one might think. In fact, in queer years, I am very, very old. I remember double-clapping to Bonnie Pointer.

In the gay male world, age is an affliction along the lines of advanced leprosy, while in Lesbo Land growing old is seen as a beautiful process that ensures a circle of wisdom among our sisters by allowing the young wimmin to lick from our fountain of knowledge. But most notably, age is the lesbian justification for getting fat, negative, bossy, and making everybody listen to your advice. This is why I feel perfectly warranted in offering a wellspring of my empirical findings on raw dating materials:

GOOD WOMEN / BAD CHOICES

1) Slacker Grrrl Dykes

A Slacker Dyke is anguished about everything. No one understands her. While one may say, "Of course nobody understands you, you're always sloppy drunk," this is not what the Slacker Grrrl wants to hear. She wants to hear, "Let me pay for it."

Occasionally one may be tempted to start a relationship with a Slacker Dyke. This is forgivable only if the Slacker Dyke is under twenty-one (and doesn't know any better) and *extremely* good-looking. But remember, behind every aging bar barnacle who's spent a lifetime avoiding the stress of motivation, there are the salad days spent as the budding perpetual art student.

Determining the Slacker Grrrl Dyke
Does she have a job?

While this may not always be indicative of the Slacker Dyke, the lack of gainful employment is your biggest tip-off that you may be entering into a terrifying world of squalid apartments, atonal music, and stunningly bad poetry. Go ahead, ask yourself, "How many evenings can I sit in an apartment so filthy the floor undulates, watching my new love interest move her lips while she reads the liner notes to a Tori Amos tape?"

Does she look like she could ever have a job?

If she wears nothing but unwashed statement-black in advanced stages of offensiveness, has boldly placed piercings, and sports a plea for attention hairstyle—she is a Slacker Dyke. Chances are her entire career and earning potential will peak behind the night counter of a Dunkin' Donuts.

Was she an extra in Go Fish?

You have to ask?

Where to Look
Art Schools
Performance Art Venues
Unemployment Lines
Behind the Pyramid of Empty Beer Cans at the Local Dyke Bar

2) Bisexual Girls

Bisexuality is a field trip for straight girls. It's an opportunity to "explore" their lesbian side. Remember the time the whole fourth grade boarded the bus to spend the day at the Holsum bakery? Did any of us ever use this experience as the impetus to become a baker? Think about it.

Before you become the destination for a straight-girl field trip, weigh all pros and cons. Yes, it will undoubtedly be highly exciting to be her first foray into the lesbian world, but on the other hand it will probably be pretty humiliating to be the maid of honor at her wedding.

Determining the Bisexual Girl

Does she have a boyfriend?

The clues don't get any bigger than this. And if you've ever spent untold torturous hours wrestling a lover away from her not-quite-ex-girlfriend, simply imagine the drama of recreating those memorable moments with a not-quite-ex-boyfriend.

Is she indecisive?

Anyone who would express an "ambivalence" about something as intrinsic as their sexuality is going to have a problem with any kind of commitment. Indeed, if she's not really sure she's a lesbian today, tomorrow she may well wonder if she's actually a woman.

Is she male-identified?

An inordinate number of straight male friends may signal a fanatical interest in discussing pro football, but more than likely it means the woman in question feels most comfortable when surrounded by men. This is not how lesbians spend a lot of time. She is not going to make a good lesbian.

Where to Look
"Gay Night" in a Straight Bar
In the Produce Section Agonizing over Which Kind of Lettuce to Buy
Women's Studies Classes
NOW Meetings

3) PC Wimmobyn

While working toward basic human rights for lesbians and female minorities is an extremely worthwhile endeavor, when accompanied by plans to phase out the male of the species, force veganism, and revel in being truly overweight, the whole thing becomes rather unpractical and unpleasant. Up to now, Political Correctness is single-handedly responsible for encouraging the odd spelling of perfectly acceptable words, renaming perfectly acceptable minority groups, and the absence of public toilets in Manhattan. I think they've done enough.

Determining the PC Wommobyn

Is there an inverse ratio between her surface area and its covering?

Cracked by the strain of having lived too long "under the male-dominated fashion industry that condemns women to a madonna/whore status by subjugating them to the role of anorexic," PC Dykes revel in showing their fat to the world. They are proud to pendulate in any wide open space, including your apartment. If you're tempted to have one over, cover and reinforce the furniture.

Is she female-identified?

PC Gurls tend to travel in huge wimmin packs that are forever meeting to complain, make rules, and plan world dominance. This will never happen, however, because no matter how brilliant the PC plan becomes, by the time it is translated into every known language, braille, ASCII, sign language, large type, wheelchair-accessible transcripts, Esperanto, pictures for the illiterate, Native American smoke signals, and African American vernacular, the world will be over anyway.

Is she hypersensitive to every odor except the one emanating from the forty-three cats living in her house?

PC Wimmin will not tolerate the smell of smoke, perfume, bonfires, car exhaust, or roasting meat. Essentially, any odor associated with a good time will be agony for the PC Dyke and she will make this known to both you and those in a three-mile radius. The ideal poetic death for a PC Wymon is spontaneous combustion. Unfortunately this all too rarely happens.

Where to Look
Wimmin's Music Festivals
Campgrounds
The Nondairy Dessert Toppings Aisle
Worshipping the Moon

GOOD WOMEN/GOOD CHOICES

1) Lipstick Lesbians
Lipstick Lesbians are on the whole a fun group. They will be impressed by any gift that glitters, and will sincerely consider a relationship to be any situation that incorporates the sharing of Revlon products. Like simple natives in other cultures, shiny things and trinkets can be offered to the Lipstick Lesbian and traded for commodities ranging from sex to their place in the bathroom line. While not emotionally deep, a relationship with a Lipstick Girl is inherently a win/win situation for any dyke with a rhinestone collection.

Determining the Lipstick Lesbian

Does she carry a purse?

This is not a femme thang, this is a practicality thang. When one is predisposed to carrying around forty pounds of facial enhancements, one is advised to carry a purse.

If you are seeking a Lipstick Lesbian, ask the woman in question for a light; if the answer to this simple request is forty minutes of rumbling through a large handbag, your search is over.

Can the time variance between "getting ready to leave" and "leaving" be measured in hours?

Lengthy preparation time for an evening out should not be viewed as indecisiveness. These women know exactly what they are doing—

they are making a new person. This takes time, concentration, creativity, and more time. Do not rush them—there is nothing more terrifying than a half-formed Lipstick Lesbian.

Does she have more fashion magazines than your closest gay male friend?

If you have previously been hanging out with garden variety lesbians, you will have noticed that their fashion magazine selections run along the lines of the Lands' End catalog and old *Playboys*. Lipstick Lesbians, however, will subscribe to more fashion magazines than a seventeen-year-old straight girl. In addition to providing reading material while waiting for her to get ready, this will also give you the opportunity to discover just the right eyebrow arch for the shape of your face.

Where to Look
The Clinique Counter
In Front of the Mirror in the Powder Room
Melissa Etheridge Concerts

2) Writer Girls
A Writer Girl is low-maintenance to the point of being a houseplant. On an average day she will spend eight hours staring at the world and another eight hours staring at her word processor. Because of a fanatical need to examine an emotion, review the reaction to an emotion, then write and rewrite for just the right emotional tone, you will never have to worry about embarrassing spontaneous outbursts. Cut them and they won't bleed. They'll write about bleeding.

The beauty of a Writer Girl relationship is in its simplicity. Searching for just the right love gift? Pick up a six-pack and cigarettes on the way home and she will be profoundly touched by your sensitivity. Feel like a reckless affair with another woman? Simply don't come home for a few weeks; by the time the Writer Girl has noticed and fashioned an emotional response, the two of you will have broken up years ago.

Determining the Writer Girl

Does she look like she just got up?

There are two reasons that the Writer Girl's physical appearance may be less than socially acceptable: 1) She is an artiste and not bound by such man-made constraints as time, hair-brushing, or shopping for clothes in this decade. 2) She just got up.

Is "bizarre" a polite word for her friends?

Writers are by nature observers and tend to collect vicarious existences through friendships. While having a heroin addict know you on a first-name basis may be a tad icky, think of your rise in party status as having personally known this year's serial killer before he was caught.

Is her longest job tenure five months?

Most businesses do not consider an employee who would rather write about working than actually work a valuable asset to the company. However, by the time an employer discovers this flaw, the Writer Girl will have made off with innumerable reams of paper, office supplies, computer components, and pirated software, which is the real reason she took the job in the first place. Subsequently, you will benefit by never being at a loss for a stapler.

Where to Look
Book Signings
Visitors' Lounge at the Mental Home
The End of the Bar
Any Convenience Market that Sells Both Cigarettes and Liquor

Good Women / Choice Choices

1) Professional Sports Stars and Celebrities

Face it, relationships just don't last. And when they do—they turn ugly. In tandem, you and life's partner will get fat, crabby, sexless, and undoubtedly end up raising little yappy dogs as a pathetic familial surrogate.

Sure, a breakup is, well, heartbreaking, but when compared to what a twenty-year relationship becomes, even the most commitment-identified can see that change is good. So, if you're going to be heartbroken anyway, why not make it worth your time? Many women, just like you, have had the pain of a breakup severely lessened with settlement accoutrements like diamond tennis bracelets and horse farms.

Determining the Sports Star/Celebrity

Is she athletically gifted?

This applies to women who are not opposed to dating younger, *much younger,* women. Unfortunately, the big-money women's sports stars, i.e., tennis players, tend to peak at an early age. On the plus side, you will be dating a woman with more money than God whose biggest dream will be buying her own pony. As you will be the only one with a license, remind her that you will drive her to the pony farm in the BMW just as soon as she buys it for you.

Does she own her own plane?

If she does, this is the equivalent of a three-cherry jackpot in Lesbian Las Vegas. Once you have established yourself as a premium chippy, life is just one big gold mine. Might I remind you that k.d., Madonna, and Sandra all have at least one thing in common—and it's not fame . . .

Does she have a contract with a television network?

This is an iffy area. While you may immediately recognize her as a dyke, America may not. There is good chance that you will be reduced to her "close personal friend," "female assistant," or "gal pal" in the press.

Where to Look
Aspen
Women's Pro Sporting Events
Backstage
On Stage
Places You Can't Get Into

Analyzing the Art of Love

Museum of Contemporary Art

237 East Ontario Street Chicago, IL 60611

Radical Scavenger(s) The Conceptual Vernacular in Recent American Art

Tuesday

(Free Admission Day)

Pre-, During, and Slightly Post-Lunch Hour

Steps from Michigan Avenue, the MCA is far enough from area schools to deflect alcoholic art students in their 30s who've never endorsed a paycheck, but close enough to Chicago advertising venues to attract cute advertising creatives looking for the concept to clinch that $45M account and access that 15% bonus.

Star Fuckers

A special comparative assessment of "celebrity" types visible at the MCA (for those of you who continue to live only for the pathetic hope that one night Jodie Foster will show up at a lezzie bar and ask you to dance), and a brief hypothesis as to what a potential relationship could garner the aggressive dating initiator.

8: Key

The k.d.:

Oh-so-hip androgyny look will quickly become passé, then vaguely reminiscent of beer-gutted dykes attached to truckers' wallets and big bunches of keys—however, your car will never run better.

The Melissa:

The ensuing tortured, obsessive relationship, fraught with odd genderless metaphors, will only be slightly outweighed by the savings realized in splitting the cost of Revlon and Clinique products.

The Martina:

High-roller relationship and eventual messy breakup virtually guarantees massive tell-all book advance and—perhaps—custody of a horse farm.

Analyzing the Art of Love

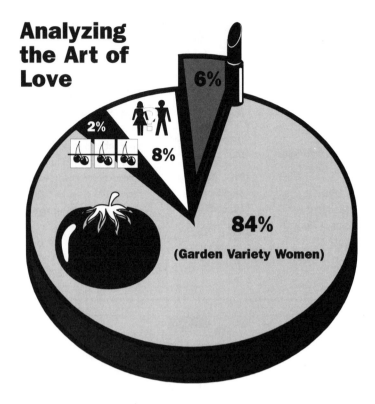

6%

2%

8%

84%
(Garden Variety Women)

11:45 AM
Have pleasant conversation with docent who is, unfortunately, male.

12:10 PM
Peering at an enigmatic display of glass paperweights ask attractive woman what she thinks; she thinks cold stare and raised eyebrow are an appropriate response.

12:34 PM
Pop into video area where 55-minute movie is in progress. Smile weakly at huge woman mesmerized by looped image of Patti Smith screeching, "Fuck God." Politely leave.

1:15 PM
Surrounded by towering images of American iconography and replicas of roadside signs, ask gorgeous blonde how it affects her, she replies—in German. In a moment of frustration I inquire, perhaps a bit too loudly, how the fuck any of this can mean anything if one doesn't speak the language. Formerly pleasant docent asks me to leave...

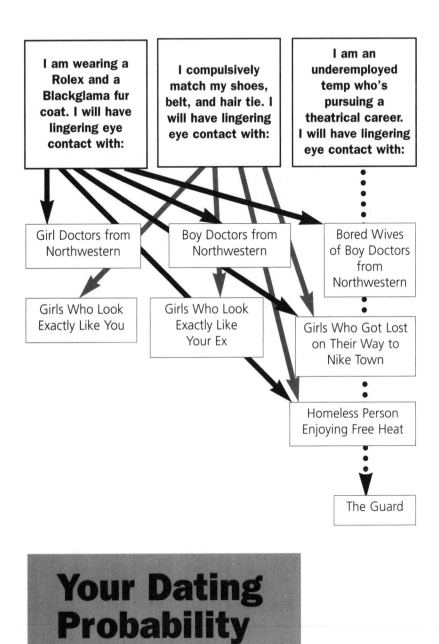

I am wearing a Rolex and a Blackglama fur coat. I will have lingering eye contact with:

I compulsively match my shoes, belt, and hair tie. I will have lingering eye contact with:

I am an underemployed temp who's pursuing a theatrical career. I will have lingering eye contact with:

Girl Doctors from Northwestern

Boy Doctors from Northwestern

Bored Wives of Boy Doctors from Northwestern

Girls Who Look Exactly Like You

Girls Who Look Exactly Like Your Ex

Girls Who Got Lost on Their Way to Nike Town

Homeless Person Enjoying Free Heat

The Guard

Your Dating Probability

Marie, owing to any number of past transgressions and personality flaws, is perpetually bereft of a date. Short of being a naked cook in a women's prison, one would assume Chicago's Capricorn Party—the absolute biggest Lesbo House Fête of the season—would be date destiny for Marie. Ha!

The most Marie was able to obtain at the party was an even greater understanding of lesbian signage. What the signs say, and what the dykes *heard the signs saying,* are often open to wide interpretation.

Girl

What the
sign said =

What the
sign meant =

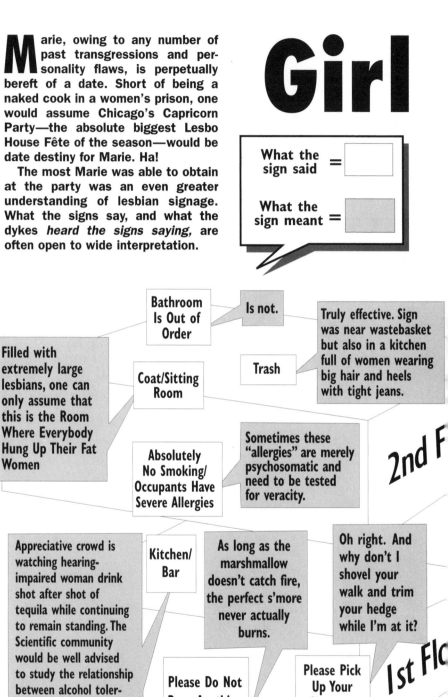

Bathroom
Is Out of
Order

Is not.

Truly effective. Sign was near wastebasket but also in a kitchen full of women wearing big hair and heels with tight jeans.

Trash

Filled with extremely large lesbians, one can only assume that this is the Room Where Everybody Hung Up Their Fat Women

Coat/Sitting
Room

Absolutely
No Smoking/
Occupants Have
Severe Allergies

Sometimes these "allergies" are merely psychosomatic and need to be tested for veracity.

2nd Fl

Appreciative crowd is watching hearing-impaired woman drink shot after shot of tequila while continuing to remain standing. The Scientific community would be well advised to study the relationship between alcohol tolerance and deafness.

Kitchen/
Bar

As long as the marshmallow doesn't catch fire, the perfect s'more never actually burns.

Oh right. And why don't I shovel your walk and trim your hedge while I'm at it?

Please Do Not
Burn Anything
in Fireplace

Please Pick
Up Your
Cigarette
Butts

1st Flo

Party

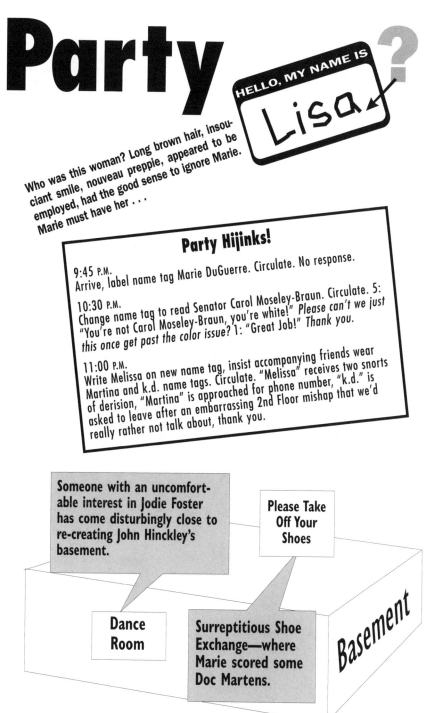

HELLO, MY NAME IS

Lisa

Who was this woman? Long brown hair, insouciant smile, nouveau preppie, appeared to be employed, had the good sense to ignore Marie. Marie must have her . . .

Party Hijinks!

9:45 P.M.
Arrive, label name tag Marie DuGuerre. Circulate. No response.

10:30 P.M.
Change name tag to read Senator Carol Moseley-Braun. Circulate. 5: "You're not Carol Moseley-Braun, you're white!" *Please can't we just this once get past the color issue?* 1: "Great Job!" *Thank you.*

11:00 P.M.
Write Melissa on new name tag, insist accompanying friends wear Martina and k.d. name tags. Circulate. "Melissa" receives two snorts of derision, "Martina" is approached for phone number, "k.d." is asked to leave after an embarrassing 2nd Floor mishap that we'd really rather not talk about, thank you.

Someone with an uncomfortable interest in Jodie Foster has come disturbingly close to re-creating John Hinckley's basement.

Please Take Off Your Shoes

Dance Room

Surreptitious Shoe Exchange—where Marie scored some Doc Martens.

Basement

⊖ Venue

Private Party
Nice Apartment
Chichi
Neighborhood

⊖ Time

Friday
8:30 P.M.–1:00 A.M.

⊖ Annotation

A gathering of approximately 20 professional women with a mean individual income approaching a refreshing $75,000. This average is later wildly skewed by the appearance of an unemployed art student whom everybody assumes somebody else invited.

⊖ Process Summary of Social Intercourse

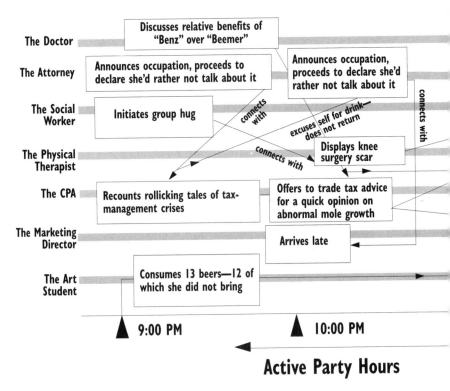

The Doctor

Discusses relative benefits of "Benz" over "Beemer"

The Attorney

Announces occupation, proceeds to declare she'd rather not talk about it

Announces occupation, proceeds to declare she'd rather not talk about it

The Social Worker

Initiates group hug

connects with

excuses self for drink does not return

The Physical Therapist

connects with

Displays knee surgery scar

connects with

The CPA

Recounts rollicking tales of tax-management crises

Offers to trade tax advice for a quick opinion on abnormal mole growth

The Marketing Director

Arrives late

The Art Student

Consumes 13 beers—12 of which she did not bring

▲ 9:00 PM   ▲ 10:00 PM

Active Party Hours

Processing the Party Process

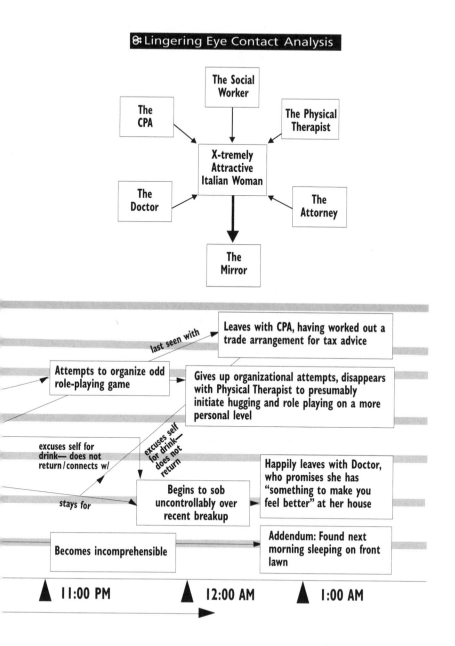

8: Lingering Eye Contact Analysis

The Social Worker

The CPA

The Physical Therapist

X-tremely Attractive Italian Woman

The Doctor

The Attorney

The Mirror

Leaves with CPA, having worked out a trade arrangement for tax advice

last seen with

Attempts to organize odd role-playing game

Gives up organizational attempts, disappears with Physical Therapist to presumably initiate hugging and role playing on a more personal level

excuses self for drink— does not return/connects w/

excuses self for drink— does not return

stays for

Begins to sob uncontrollably over recent breakup

Happily leaves with Doctor, who promises she has "something to make you feel better" at her house

Becomes incomprehensible

Addendum: Found next morning sleeping on front lawn

11:00 PM   12:00 AM   1:00 AM

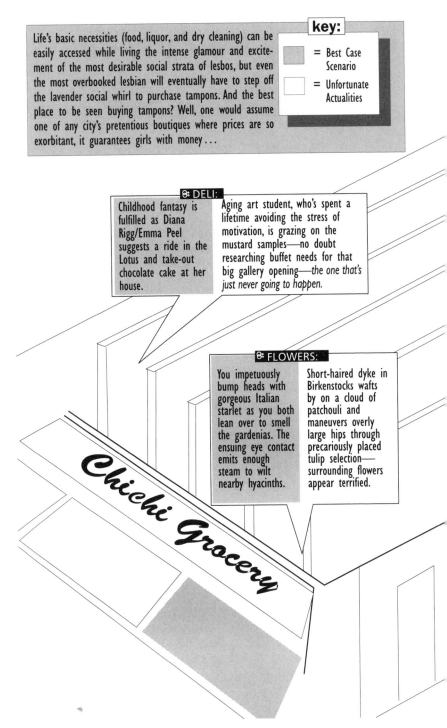

Life's basic necessities (food, liquor, and dry cleaning) can be easily accessed while living the intense glamour and excitement of the most desirable social strata of lesbos, but even the most overbooked lesbian will eventually have to step off the lavender social whirl to purchase tampons. And the best place to be seen buying tampons? Well, one would assume one of any city's pretentious boutiques where prices are so exorbitant, it guarantees girls with money...

key:

☐ = Best Case Scenario

☐ = Unfortunate Actualities

☞ DELI:

Childhood fantasy is fulfilled as Diana Rigg/Emma Peel suggests a ride in the Lotus and take-out chocolate cake at her house.

Aging art student, who's spent a lifetime avoiding the stress of motivation, is grazing on the mustard samples—no doubt researching buffet needs for that big gallery opening—*the one that's just never going to happen.*

☞ FLOWERS:

You impetuously bump heads with gorgeous Italian starlet as you both lean over to smell the gardenias. The ensuing eye contact emits enough steam to wilt nearby hyacinths.

Short-haired dyke in Birkenstocks wafts by on a cloud of patchouli and maneuvers overly large hips through precariously placed tulip selection—surrounding flowers appear terrified.

Chichi Grocery

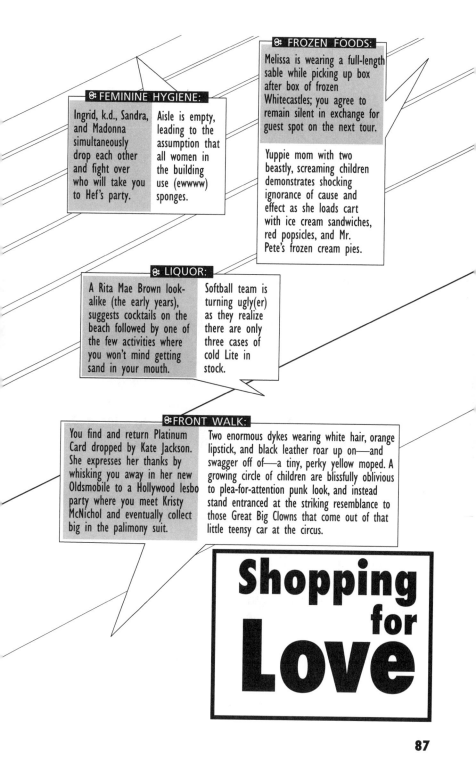

FROZEN FOODS:

Melissa is wearing a full-length sable while picking up box after box of frozen Whitecastles; you agree to remain silent in exchange for guest spot on the next tour.

Yuppie mom with two beastly, screaming children demonstrates shocking ignorance of cause and effect as she loads cart with ice cream sandwiches, red popsicles, and Mr. Pete's frozen cream pies.

FEMININE HYGIENE:

Ingrid, k.d., Sandra, and Madonna simultaneously drop each other and fight over who will take you to Hef's party.

Aisle is empty, leading to the assumption that all women in the building use (ewwww) sponges.

LIQUOR:

A Rita Mae Brown look-alike (the early years), suggests cocktails on the beach followed by one of the few activities where you won't mind getting sand in your mouth.

Softball team is turning ugly(er) as they realize there are only three cases of cold Lite in stock.

FRONT WALK:

You find and return Platinum Card dropped by Kate Jackson. She expresses her thanks by whisking you away in her new Oldsmobile to a Hollywood lesbo party where you meet Kristy McNichol and eventually collect big in the palimony suit.

Two enormous dykes wearing white hair, orange lipstick, and black leather roar up on—and swagger off of—a tiny, perky yellow moped. A growing circle of children are blissfully oblivious to plea-for-attention punk look, and instead stand entranced at the striking resemblance to those Great Big Clowns that come out of that little teensy car at the circus.

Shopping for Love

Dyke Drama

esbian relationships are never confined to two people. They are vast sharing forums dedicated to breaking up, re-forming, and talk, talk, talking about it. It is not uncommon to attend a large party and realize you've had a relationship, either intimately or vicariously, with everyone in attendance, including the catering personnel.

Despite the ick-factor, there is a consolation to this: If one lives long enough, one will know the peculiarities of every existing lesbian and exactly how the breakup will come—well before the first date.

When you are going through that inevitable parting, you will talk about it to the point of tedium. In kind, you will be consoled with any number of tedious comfort-phrases, such as: "Things fall into place," "It's for the best," "Man, that sucks for you," or "Hey DuGuerre, you're up!"

From the files of my personal experience, I can offer an ordeal involving a breakup with a former long-term object of my affections, the new object of her affections (a person quite low on the food chain), and a scenario straight out of hell in which I was unaccountably stalked by the latter. I was so miserable I drank all the time. No, wait a minute: I was *so* miserable, I *couldn't* drink all the time.

How did I cope? What comfort-mechanism did I come up with? Well, at a point of complete demoralization I cut out a smarmy Ann Landers column and made *My Recipe for Happiness.* Then I sent it to the person that was stalking me, and they never bothered me again:

My Recipe for Happiness

You Will Need:
Soap Flakes
1 Gallon Rubber Cement
$^1/_2$ Gallon Gasoline
Large *plastic* bucket

Empty rubber cement into bucket. Thoroughly mix rubber cement with sifted soap flakes until they form a slightly dry, jell-like consistency. Slowwwly pour gasoline into . . . *Hey! This isn't My Recipe for Happiness, this is my recipe for napalm—whoops.*

It seems I've misplaced my recipe for happiness, which means that . . . Oh my, but this explains a lot.

Well, suffice to say that **MY RECIPE FOR NAPALM** can also go a long way in relieving the stress of unbearable breakups.

• •

What You're Missing by Not Being Deaf

et's be realistic, signers at a women's concert simply cannot translate every single word of a song that is often incomprehensible even to the hearing. And most certainly the aural subtleties—such as Ms. Etheridge conveying that she really, *really* needs some water, or ms. lang artfully smearing the word "mental" across four syllables—are lost on the hearing impaired no matter how conscientious the signer. In fact, translation of a lyric such as "big-boned gal from Southern Alberta" could, in the interest of brevity, become "fat Canadian woman" and still remain remarkably true to the original lyric. So why labor over a complicated metaphor for dysfunctional obsession when "needy" is so much easier to sign and infinitely more apt? Indeed.

This is not to say the hearing impaired don't enjoy their own optical subtext . . .

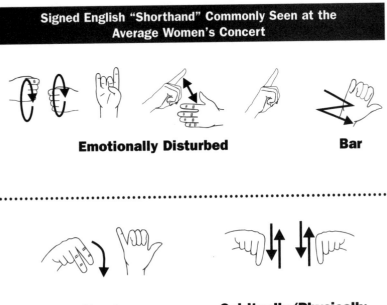

Signed English "Shorthand" Commonly Seen at the Average Women's Concert

Emotionally Disturbed   **Bar**

Needy   **Spiritually/Physically Crippled**

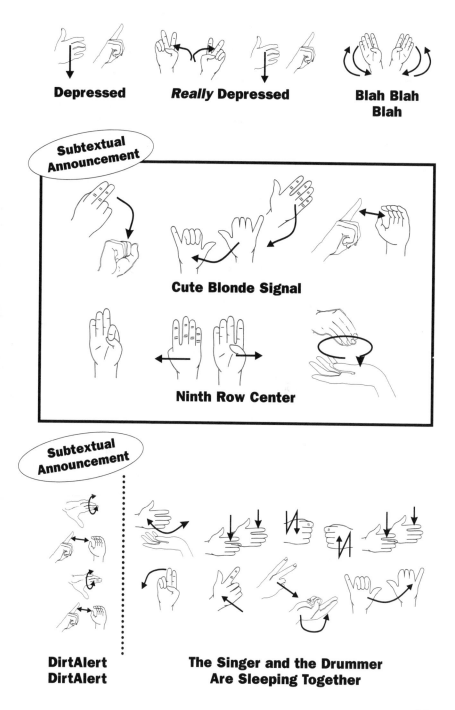

Depressed

***Really* Depressed**

**Blah Blah
Blah**

Subtextual
Announcement

Cute Blonde Signal

Ninth Row Center

Subtextual
Announcement

**DirtAlert
DirtAlert**

**The Singer and the Drummer
Are Sleeping Together**

the rites of Spring

Hey! It's January! And you know what that means—only four more months to softball season! Marie invites you to put on some shorts, sit on the radiator, close your eyes, and imagine a warm breeze. Now picture some of the biggest women God ever made stampeding through the local park. Voilà! Spring softball. And if that doesn't complete your anticipation of the biggest rite of spring, catch a couple of hours of Sumo wrestling on ESPN.

FOB: A Comparative Analysis in Poundage

A true comprehension of the sheer bulk of a women's softball team is only accessible to a handful of Nobel Prize–winners and George Lucas, creator of Jabba the Hut. For the edification of the layperson, the weight of an average team has been converted to poundage loaded on an eighteen-wheeler headed for the ultimate destination of Provincetown, MA. At the going rate of $6 per pound per 100 miles, the cost of moving a ten-woman team from Chicago will perhaps give some insight into the immensity of this endeavor as well as other imponderables, such as moving the Barnum & Bailey Circus, floating the Queen Mary, and calculating lift-off fuel for the Goodyear Blimp.

Average Weight of Player: <u>**200 pounds**</u>
(× a minimum of 10 players, equals:)

Average Weight of Team: <u>**2,000 pounds**</u> **(1 ton)**

	Weight Addition	Cost to Hart, MI	Cost to Northampton, MA	Cost to Provincetown, MA
The Team	n/a	$25,808.00	$112,560.00	**$125,520.00**
+ Dogs	310 lbs	$3,887.40	$17,446.80	**$19,455.60**
+ Girlfriends	2,000 lbs	$25,808.00	$112,560.00	**$125,520.00**
+ Beer	2,000 lbs	$25,808.00	$112,560.00	**$125,520.00**
+ Emotional Baggage	n/a except in the heavy toll on driver's mental health	growing expenditure in driver patience	driver-tolerance outlay registers a deficit as team begins "200,000 Bottles of Beer" sing-along	emotionally spent, driver will exhibit, for the rest of his natural life, a taste for lite beer and a nervous tic whenever k.d. lang is heard
GRAND TOTAL		**$81,311.40**	**$355,126.80**	**$396,015.60**

Hypotheticals:

Probable effects of 10-woman team simultaneously falling off of:

an airplane
Ranch house in the suburbs receives a new basement

the wagon
Impossible, as it presupposes being *on* the wagon—the ultimate infraction of the sacred softball-girl pledge

bar stools at the local dyke bar*
Jukebox selection "YMCA" skips to "I Will Always Love You"—crowd continues singing

high heels
It is to laugh . . .

*empirical data—has actually happened

The Language of Love

Marie travels extensively. She finds nothing more fulfilling than shamelessly lying about herself while pursuing vacation romances. As Marie is dark-haired with good teeth, she often passes herself off as a Kennedy. Because no one knows just how many Kennedys there are, she is rarely caught. In addition to skillful prevarication, Marie is adept at the Universal Language of Love. Actually, Marie is most fluent in the Universal Language of Imposition, but she would like to share with you one phrase she can repeat in any language . . .

French:

Oui, vous êtes très jolie, mais où est Catherine Deneuve?
Yes, you are very pretty, but where is Catherine Deneuve?

Spanish:

Sí, usted es muy bonita, pero ¿dónde está Gloria Estefan?
Yes, you are very pretty, but where is Gloria Estefan?

Sign Language:

Yes, you are very pretty, but where is Marlee Matlin?

Smoke Signals:

Yes, you are very pretty, but where is Pocahontas?

Semaphore:

Yes, you are very pretty, but where is The Little Mermaid?

• •

The Search for Validation

HOWARD STREET
GROCERY & GUN

YOUR CASHIER...ELLEN
CUST 95 REG 12 OPR 177
STORE 534

4CARTON/WINSCIG
DELI/
  PÂTÉ
  CORNED BEEF
  VEAL
  BABY RBIT HRTS
COSMETICS/
  DUKLNG I-LINER
  42OZ HAIRSPRY
AMMO/
  1BX HLLW PTS
LIQUOR/CASE COORS

The Fur Vault
we'll save your skin...

1 white seal-stroller
1 fox full-length
1 baby kitten earmuffs

Claim #: A001345-6435

NIGAZ IN HOODZ
The
Cap Cops/ Rape Ho's/Wear Funny Clothes
Tour
VIP PASS with Special Guest **VIP PASS**
Louis Farrakan

Did you ever do something *really* stupid?

Like, say, you're in the middle of a crowded line at a very politically correct fund-raiser? And maybe you're searching through your purse for your parking stub so you can get it validated? Then, like, your entire purse spills on the floor? And, perhaps, as everyone scrambles to pick up your items, you realize that there is *a lot* of stuff in your purse that could really ruin your chances for *any* kind of social acceptance? All while you notice that an uncomfortable hush has fallen over the crowd?

Me neither.

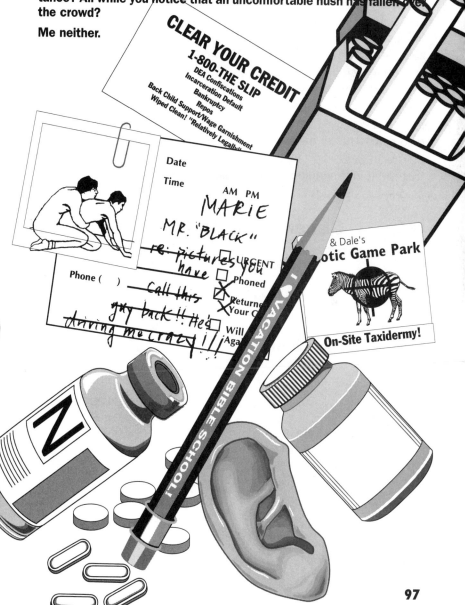

CLEAR YOUR CREDIT
1-800-THE SLIP
DEA Confiscations
Incarceration Default
Bankruptcy
Back Child Support/Wage Garnishment
Repos
Wiped Clean! "Relatively Legal!"

Date

Time

AM PM

MARIE
MR. "BLACK"
re: pictures you
have
Call this
guy back!! He's
driving me crazy!!!

Phone (   )

☐ URGENT
☐ Phoned
☒ Returned Your C
☒ Will
   Aga

& Dale's
otic Game Park
On-Site Taxidermy!

I ♥ VACATION BIBLE SCHOOL!

Anybody Got a
Quaalude?

Despite the smiley-faced "We Are Everywhere" queer credo, there are a few locales where happenin' homos should feel decidedly uncomfortable—the rifle range at boot camp, Pentecostal church services, the Wisconsin Dells in August, and queer bars in suburban strip malls.

For example, the kind of bar Marie recently visited in suburban Franklin "The Land the '90s Forgot" Park. Not so much a bar as a vast excavation of '80s memorabilia. A storehouse of disco music, big hair, gold chains, glitter balls, girls in Izod shirts with the collar turned up, boys with precision dance interpretations of "Gloria." Basically a bar that revels in everything but the reason we acted that way in the first place—lots of drugs.

General Patron Makeup

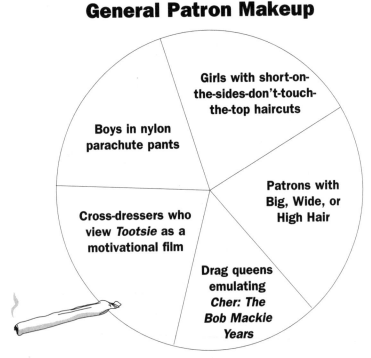

Girls with short-on-the-sides-don't-touch-the-top haircuts

Boys in nylon parachute pants

Patrons with Big, Wide, or High Hair

Cross-dressers who view *Tootsie* as a motivational film

Drag queens emulating *Cher: The Bob Mackie Years*

Answers to Marie's question: "Have you got any poppers?"

"What?"
"That stuff's bad for you."
"It's illegal."
"Wow! You've done poppers?!"

Phrases Marie actually heard in 1996:

"This is tuff."
"Can I buy you a brew?"
"She's a fox."
"I'm just TCBing, babe."

Musical relics Marie actually saw people dance to:

Flock of Seagulls
KajaGooGoo
The Pet Shop Boys
Lisa Lisa and the
 Cult Jam
Nu Shooz
M Tune

Suppositions
Predicted Percentage of Patrons Who:

have copies of *Xanadu*, *Footloose,* and *Flashdance* on Betamax   **65%**

own a puka-shell necklace   **35%**

sleep on a waterbed   **24%**

subscribe to a fashion magazine   **0%**

Christmas Shopping

Artistes

Observing the fashion sense, hygiene, and social graces of the average girl painters, singers, and poets, one could easily assume they spent their formative years living with gypsy wolves shunned by the rest of the pack for their bad taste. Don't be fooled—these girls *choose* to live this way. Honest, just ring up Daddy in the burbs and tell him his daughter cheated you in a drug deal—he'll tell you all about it . . .

Buy:
Berets
Atonal Girl-Singer Music
Food and Basic Necessities
Easily Pawned Items

Avoid:
Personal Hygiene Products
Lingerie Drawer Sachets
Self-Help Books
Anything that Requires Electricity
Childproof Items
Anything with Instructions

Captainettes of Industry

Serious women, serious money, serious gift competition. The idea here is not to give actual useful items, but one-up everyone else in the uniqueness of the gift. So, if you have neither the time nor the inclination to fashion a "Mayan Fetish" from a rusty coat hanger and present it as authentic, find something . . . well, something *serious*.

Buy:
Excessive Luxury Items that Can Be Operated from a Benz Cigarette Lighter

Exotic Cellular Phone Accoutrement

Piquant Cheeses and Wines from Previously Unknown Regions of the World

Any Art Object that Can Be Referred To as "An Enigmatic Piece"

Avoid:
Entertainment Coupon Books
American Brand Names
Hummel Figurines
Avon Skin-So-Soft
Anything with Feathers

A s with everything else that used to be fun, the breeders have turned Christmas shopping into a queer's nightmare. What used to be a couple of hooty afternoons spent actively bossing around the uptight retail staff with your gay-boy friends has turned into some hideous hell on earth. A recent fifteen minutes at the mall assaulted every refined gay sensibility and resulted in our entire group beating such a hasty retreat that there was a near fatal breeder/stroller pileup in the shoe department. Another ten minutes and our frown wrinkles may have been permanent. Yes, shopping conditions were so heinous, *even the gay men complained.*

What follows is my Guide to Gay-Girl Gift Giving. Simple, easy-to-follow, and annoyingly alliterative, it targets four common lesbo types and details what they want for Christmas. It will have you in and out of the mall in no time. (If only relationships were this easy to figure out.)

Social Gals

Lesbians incorporate more social workers per capita than any other group. If you don't have at least one overly earnest friend working in social services, you are not really a lesbian. Driving in their neighborhoods, one can practically hydroplane on the gooey nurturing that fills the street. Of course the best gift for these carin' 'n' sharin' types would be peace on earth and worldwide vegetarianism, but since one's ability to find these items in the correct size is severely limited, stick to something warm, fuzzy, and slightly sticky.

Buy:

Things with Feathers
Whimsical Cat Toys
Useless Items Made by an Oppressed Group
Free-Range Wool Apparel (earth tones)
Poignant Wind Chimes (meditative tones)
Kittens (miniature cat tones)

Avoid:

Guns
Furs
Live Lobster Grams

Burb Babes

The suburbs are an excuse to have a house with a yard for the dogs. Dykes in the burbs ALWAYS have dogs. They are usually trapped in some psychotic marriage that is so stifling they are forced to heighten their hair and go to lame suburban bars for some semblance of fun, or they've just left some psychotic marriage that is going to take years to get over. Never, ever, get involved with a lesbo that lives in the burbs. However, Xmas shopping for burb dykes is ever so easy. Think yard. Think dogs. Think yaawwwwnnnnn . . .

Buy:

Art that Coordinates with the Sofa
The Crock-Pot Cookbook
Sears Craftsman Lawn Care Products
Anything—no matter how inane—with a Pro Sports Team Logo
Comical Dog Toys

Avoid:

Anything "Funky"
Brand Names that Are Difficult to Pronounce
Items that Presume a Sex Life

V-A-C-A-T-I-O-N
in the Winter Sun

Chicago being what it is—God's refrigerator—allows us an eight-month window of opportunity for taking a winter vacation. (Marie personally recommends Quintana Roo in southern Mexico for the winter. Everybody there is so godawful poor that simply eating once a day seems super-giddy-fun by comparison. It is extremely difficult not to have a successful vacation in Quintana Roo.)

This year, Marie went to Key West. Florida. Purgatory. As in the huge Dante-esque waiting room for Cuban refugees, a cozy tropic vestibule for many species awaiting extinction and for old people, the toasty foyer to death.

Like moths to a tiki torch, gays are drawn to any situation that appears to be so fun it could kill you. Given Key West's physical proximity to Hell, and its mental proximity to the Disco Years, it is easy to see why so many gays vacation there.

The Venue	Fashion	Subtle Ways of Keeping Us in Line
Key West is a lot like New Orleans without the potential of running into '90s-kinda-gal Anne Rice. In Key West, you face the possibility of stumbling across '80s-has-been Kelly McGillis. I think maybe Morgan Fairchild lives there too; if not, she should. Key West calls itself the Conch Republic in a fanciful display of secession from the U.S. If you want to annoy absolutely everybody, pronounce "conch" to rhyme with "raunch" at every opportunity. My companion amused herself for hours doing this, and when gently reminded by retail staff of the correct pronunciation would angrily demand to speak to the head "honk-o" about their attitude. As they appeared to be in short supply, I strongly considered using teeth as a form of currency among the natives. **Diversions** A queer nirvana—shopping, tanning, drinking, sex, dancing. Repeated endlessly.	There were many, many men— and no dearth of women— who perpetuated the Ernest "Papa" Hemingway look. Portly, bearded, prone to suspendered walking shorts and beer-stained button-downs—this is not a good look for anyone except maybe overrated dead writers with shotgun holes in their heads who are moldering in their graves where no one can see them. The concierge at my meet-the-insect-world-in-your-cottage was wearing recently purchased skin-tight jeans pegged at the ankle, with five-inch zippers in the back. This was accented by an acrylic sweater with a sailor collar. The apparel of the late '70s and early '80s appeared to represent a peak epoch for a number of the locals. The puzzling thing is where they found all those clothes *new*. Vacationers were extremely easy to spot; in defiance of what had to be a state law, they tended to employ fashion from this decade.	There is only one road into, and out of, Key West. If something should happen to a section of that road, one would be trapped with a startling percentage of America's gay male population on a very, very tiny island. The specter of this possibility and its consequences—oh my God, the whining!—dictated that the intelligent lesbian never spend the night on Key West. Disco music plays nonstop. In Key West, Donna Summer perseveres as a toot-toot beep-beep Bad Girl, Gloria Gaynor survives twenty-four hours a day, and Grace Jones is still incomprehensible. "Jump Shout," "You Dropped a Bomb on Me," "The Electric Slide"—all of the songs that made the early '80s a huge glitter ball of excess are forever blasting from all points. And all of it seems carefully orchestrated to keep gays twirling, twirling, twirling and at last, like that ballerina in *The Red Shoes*, send us dancing exhaustedly into the ocean, from whence we are never seen again.

Key West

My Kinda Vacation Town

I live in Chicago but sometimes pretend I'm here on vacation so that I can experience the city as authentic and charming instead of annoying and cluttered. If I were truly vacationing in Chicago, here's what I'd do:

First, I'd wait until July. By then we're all light-headed with the fact that we can be outside for extended periods of time and not die from exposure. This leads to frantic nonstop outdoor galas that all have to be crammed into that very short time before the sun god dies again. Chicago in the summer is the height of hysterical fun.

Never mind any of the usual tourist spots: The Sears Tower is—surprise!—tall, Michigan Avenue is an overpriced photo op for the world's suburbanites, and that Picasso thing in Daley Plaza is actually the pigeon mecca for North America—linger even momentarily and you will be pooped on.

If you are boy-identified, go immediately to Roscoes on Halsted. If you are girl-identified, go to The Closet on Broadway. Both of these places feature enough attitude to make either coastal visitor happy. In addition, at The Closet you can see bartender Pate's hair—an intriguing tourist attraction in itself. You will also be conveniently located in Boystown, our too-festive Bourbon Street for Queers. If you want to know about S/M, fetish, gothic, or underpants-only kind of places you'll have to ask someone else—I feel just being queer is deviant enough; anything more would be overkill.

SOME THINGS TO REMEMBER:

Public transportation in Chicago is excellent. I highly recommend that all visitors rely on public transportation, as cautious driving will result in a baseball bat injury facilitated by a hostile Chicago motorist.

However, when using public transportation there is one thing you need to know; because of huge amounts of pilferage among Chicago Transit Authority (CTA) employees, CTA personnel can no longer sell tokens. This is like the post office telling you that they don't sell stamps. A consumer must make a special trip to buy tokens from check-cashing places or convenience stores, or otherwise pay an extra quarter per fare at the turnstiles. I resent being punished by the CTA just because they have no policy against hiring felons. This makes me so angry that I regularly get back at the CTA by using centavos in the turnstiles. I once even stuffed a note into the slot that read, "Sorry about the inconvenience but I find that I steal from myself if I carry CTA tokens. If you wait until I've been through about a hundred thousand more times, you can take all those centavos to a check-cashing place and get them changed for an American dime." If you visit Chicago, bring lots of centavos.

People from the East Coast invariably find our city to be friendly to the point of naïveté—as if Chicago is some kind of Happy Camp for retarded adults. It is. For every savvy Chicago native, there are a thousand people who just left any of a thousand teensy rural towns that relied on years of inbreeding to produce the dunderpate who is now idly wandering "the big city." This person will be the charming samaritan that returns the wallet you dropped, still full of cash, and will also be the idiot that is driving an oil-burning '72 Montego two miles an hour down the middle of Michigan Avenue in front of the cab that is late in carrying you to the business appointment that would have changed your life.

If you're from the West Coast, you will be surprised at how good the food is in Chicago. Especially ethnic food. And the best food is located in areas so true to their heritage that all of the restaurant signs, menus, and speech are in languages most native Americans don't understand. Mime "hungry" to the waitress and you'll receive something so delicious you'll want to eat it every day. Too bad—as you're never really sure what you've had, you will never be able to order it again.

If you are from the East Coast, you will be astounded at the tremendous amount of good theater, and appalled at the excessive amount of bad theater. We have theaters where most people have potted plants—in Chicago an extra closet is considered an intimate-seating repertory. Everybody in Chicago theater thinks they will be the next Gary Sinise. It doesn't seem to bother them that outside of Chicago theater, nobody really knows who he is.

If you are from Los Angeles, you will be shot dead in a drive-by, as you are undoubtedly from a rival gang. Stay home.

If you are here with little money but vast pretensions, you will probably stay in Wicker Park with all of the other too-sensitive-for-employment poets, painters, and singers. Wicker Park was crafted by leisure-class artistes to suggest an area of gritty, decaying, urban squalor so that gritty, decaying talent like Liz Phair and Rose Troche could have someplace to be. Please do not leave Wicker Park, as other areas have ordinances against people like you.

· ·

Warning Signs on the Highway of Life

Life in the '90s is fraught with wishing each and every one of us such a healthy, safe, and litigation-free existence that we have labels on lawn mowers warning us not to touch the blade while it's moving.

While we may go through our lives fully warned against the temptation to blow-dry our hair in the shower, take that entire bottle of painkillers, or smoke cigarettes near gasoline, the things that can truly hurt—those emotional scars left on our psyches by psychos—go completely without advance notice.

As the dysfunction-monitors for the rest of humanity, lesbians have unaccountably overlooked the benefits of the warning label. Until now. Welcome to the new millennium—**The Age of Enforced Self-Disclosure.** Xerox the following a hundred million times and pass them out to applicable friends. Oh, and don't forget to do some personal cutting and pasting—*you know who you are.*

CAUTION

I Am So Completely Incapable of a Long-Term Relationship that I Have No Houseplants

ALARM

↓

I Have a Criminal Record

DANGER

I Have Eight Personalities, None of Whom Are Particularly Pleasant

NOTICE

Love Me, Love My Family. Every weekend for the Rest of Your Life

I Carry More Baggage than the Royal Family on Tour